ADHD

Raising an Explosive Child with a Fast Mind.

With strategies for emotional control and positive parenting to make your child feel loved.

KENNETH HARVEY

© **Copyright 2022 - All rights reserved.**

The content contained within this book may not be reproduced, duplicated, or transmitted without direct written permission from the author or the publisher.

Under no circumstances will any blame or legal responsibility be held against the publisher, or author, for any damages, reparation, or monetary loss due to the information contained within this book, either directly or indirectly.

Legal Notice:

This book is copyright protected, and it is only for personal use. You cannot amend, distribute, sell, use, quote, or paraphrase any part, or the content within this book, without the consent of the author or publisher.

Disclaimer Notice:

Please note the information contained within this document is for educational and entertainment purposes only. All effort has been executed to present accurate, up-to-date, reliable, and complete information. No warranties of any kind are declared or implied. Readers acknowledge that the author is not engaged in rendering legal, financial, medical, or professional advice. The content within this book has been derived from various sources. Please consult a licensed professional before attempting any techniques outlined in this book.

By reading this document, the reader agrees that under no circumstances is the author responsible for any losses, direct or indirect, that are incurred as a result of the use of the information contained within this document, including, but not limited to, errors, omissions, or inaccuracies.

I Dedicate These Books To My Daughter Who Has Opened My Mind To Learning More About ADHD And Encouraging Me To Write This Book To Help Other Parents Struggling To Understand ADHD.

Contents

Introduction 1

Chapter 1: What Is ADHD? 5
    What Is ADHD? 6
    Causes 7
    The ADHD Brain 8
    Types 10
        Inattentive 12
        Hyperactive-Impulsive ADHD 13
        Combined-Type ADHD 14

Chapter 2: Conditions Associated With ADHD 17
    Behavioral Conditions 17
        Oppositional Defiant Disorder 17
        Conduct Disorder 18
    Learning Disorders 19
        Dyslexia 20
        Dyscalculia 20
        Dysgraphia 20
    Mental Health 20
        Depression 21
        Anxiety 22
    Physical Health 24
        Injury Risk 24
        Staying Healthy 25
    Intensity Of Emotions: Common Causes of "Blowing Up" 26
        Flooding 26
        Criticism 27

   Fear and Anxiety 27
   Denial 28
   Caught In a Storm 28
   Low Self-Esteem 29
   Procrastination 30
   Why Do These Things Happen? 31
Management Techniques 31
   Medication 31
   Cognitive Behavioral Therapy 32
   Coaching 33
   Talking Through Intensity 34
   Some At-Home Tips 34
Managing With New School Challenges 35
What We Can Do 36
   Plan a Schedule 36
   Have Breaks 36
   Timers and Clocks 36
   Rewards 36
   Offer Support 37

Chapter 3: ADHD and Emotion Control 39
The Immediate Steps 40
   Time Them and Know 40
   Keep Track Of Strategies That Work 40
   Save The Talking for Later 40
   Get Everyone Calm 41
   Help With Emotion Identification 41
Discipline In the Face of a Meltdown 41
   Public Situations 42

    Avoid Obvious Anger *42*

    Separate *43*

    Stick To Your Guns *44*

Strategies For Emotional Balance Through the Day 44

    Describing Feelings *45*

    Having A Long Term Plan *45*

    Meditation *46*

Being Gentle With Yourself 47

Chapter 4: Good or Bad Disciplines? **49**

What To Do Before You Use a New Method 50

Your Role 50

    Establish a Routine *51*

Behaviors Outside Your Child's Control 51

Different Strategies 53

    Daily Uplifting Interactions *53*

    Careful Direction *54*

    Pay Attention to the Good Behavior and Let Your Child Know *54*

    Consequences That Are a Result Of Their Actions *54*

Extra Tips 55

    Do vs. Don't *55*

    Keep a Tally of Behavior *55*

    Keep It Visible *55*

    Show What You Are Asking *55*

    Have A Safe, Cool Down Space *56*

Chapter 5: Burn That Energy With Activities **57**

Dance Parties 57

A Scavenger Hunt 57

Create A Course With Common Items 58

Get a Balance Board 58
Playing Ball... With Balloons 58
Inside Friendly Toys That You Don't Normally Think About .. 59
Group Activities 59
Solo Sports 59
Trampoline 60
Knock Out Some Chores 60
Water Fight 60
Yoga 61
Let it Fly 61
Sculptures 61
Art 61
Take Advantage of Things In Your Community 62
Concentration Based Activities 62
   Sequencing and Matching Games 62
   Simon Says 63
   Puzzles 63
   Active Video Games 63
Older Kids 64
   Martial Arts 64
   Scavenger Hunt: Teen Addition 64
   Sports 65
   Building On Art 65
   Making Music 65
   Theater 66
   Board Games 66

Chapter 6: Nutrition and Well-Being 67
The Why and the How 68
MyPlate 69
Foods To Focus On 70
- *Complex Carbs* *70*
- *Lean Meats and Protein* *72*
- *Fats (Well, Healthy Fats)* *72*
- *Vitamins and Minerals* *73*

Foods That Your Child Should Avoid 74
- *Artificial Coloring* *74*
- *Refined Sugars and Simple Carbohydrates* *75*
- *Caffeine* *76*

Sample Diet and Best Tips 77
- *Be On the Lookout For Sensitivities and Allergies* *77*
- *Balance and Routine* *77*
- *Have Things Prepared In Advance* *78*
- *Eliminate Slowly* *78*
- *Restriction* *79*
- *Diet Idea: Mediterranean Eating Pattern* *80*

Chapter 7: ADHD Is a Superpower 81
Benefits 82
- *Hyperfocus* *82*
- *Resilience* *82*
- *Creative and Outside-the-Box Thinking* *83*
- *Conversationalist* *83*
- *Spontaneous Ideas* *84*
- *Consistent Energy* *84*

How to Make the Most Out of This 85
   Top Tips 85
   Management Ideas 86
Celebrities 86
   Simone Biles 87
   Justin Timberlake 87
   Adam Levine 87
   Channing Tatum 87
   Emma Watson 88
   Micheal Phelps 88
   Lisa Ling 88
   Will.i.am 89
   Scott Kelly 89
   Ty Pennington 89
   Karina Smirnoff 89
   Johnny Depp 90
   Richard Branson 90
   Jamie Oliver 90
   Bill Gates 90

Chapter 8: Teaching Your Child Life Skills 93
Activities and Strategies That Can Help 93
   A list for you! 93
   Create Activities Out of It 94
   Pay More Attention To What's Working 94
   Achievement Chart 94
   Start With Organization Skills ASAP 95
   Timers 95
   Be Hands-On 95

- Teenage Based Strategies 96
  - Organization 96
  - Independence 96
  - The Financial Deal 97
  - Encourage Various Relationships 97
  - A Natural Course Of Action 97
- The Skills 98
  - Increasing Independence 98
  - Time 98
  - Saving 99
  - Taking Charge of Their Meds 99
  - Decision-Making Power 99

Conclusion 101

References 103

Introduction

I closed my eyes for a moment, trying to take a deep breath and calm down. I could hear my daughter sobbing as she shoved her spelling practice away from her for the fifth time. The critiques of others were playing in my head. It wouldn't take an average child more than 20 minutes to go over a spelling test, yet we were closing in on an hour.

When my eyes opened, I found my daughter looking at me. I could see the hurt and the frustration in her eyes. She wasn't acting this way because she "just didn't want to do her homework" or thought that she would get out of what we were trying to do by misbehaving.

She was genuinely frustrated with the situation. I sat there and tried to get her back on task. I tried to redirect her attention and finish the homework before us, but it wasn't working. I tried all of the methods people said would help all of the kids, but it wasn't helping mine. Why was this happening? Was my daughter a bad kid? Was I a bad parent?

The answer to both is no.

There was something else that was creating this problem. My daughter has always been wonderful and talented. But, like so many children before her, she struggles with attention deficit hyperactivity disorder (ADHD). The methods I was using were built for children whose brain was considered typical for the average child, and my child's brain was built differently, so these methods were not registering with her.

How often have you looked at your child and watched as they just seemed to blow up? It wasn't because of poor behavior, but rather, they seemed to be fighting their internal wiring. How often have you watched as your child reacted in a way that you didn't understand? Everyone around you tells you that they need more discipline or suggests things like corporal punishment.

Introduction

The answer you get often comes with more questions that make matters worse. We are just starting to understand what ADHD entails, and doctors who diagnose are often not on top of new information because they have so many conditions to keep up with. Instead of understanding what's going on, you are left with explanations like "they just can't sit still," "they're really disruptive," or "they need more discipline." None of this advice is helpful, and it doesn't help us raise children into successful adults.

The answers to your questions have emerged in some of the latest research. You probably want to know what is going on in your kiddo's brain that makes things more challenging for them, and you probably want to know why they struggle and how you can help them.

The answers that have been found can help you! They show you the ins and outs, and they give you a path that you can take your child on to help them grow into a unique and successful adult!

I want to help you learn what tools and techniques have been developed that help children with ADHD.

First, we are going to answer a core question that you might not have been able to understand yet. Next, we will take a look at conditions and emotional states that correlate with ADHD, as well as how they might impact your child.

Once we have the basics down, we can dive in on how best to help children through their emotions. Traditional methods of discipline might not work, so we will explore other methods that don't involve tears of frustration from you or your kiddo. If you're wondering what some good ways to reach them through their ADHD might be, or if you are wondering about medication, we're going to cover that too!

Because a big part of ADHD is having a lot of energy, we will be looking at healthy and appropriate outlets. With energetic outlets comes the need for nutrition. Did you know that some foods can be detrimental to someone who has ADHD? It can make things worse! But what are those foods?

The final things we will touch on are the areas where having ADHD is a magical thing. Having ADHD is labeled as having a learning disability, but really, it often just means that you don't learn or think the same way others do, and outside of a standardized environment, this can be beautiful.

It's hard to watch our kiddos struggle. There are many areas of life, especially as children, where the world isn't friendly to those with ADHD. Despite this, your kiddo can still enter the world equipped with life skills that help them be their best.

I have only ever wanted this for my daughter. I watched as she struggled with school and with managing her ADHD. I encountered problems at every turn, which wasn't my daughter's fault. Doctors didn't seem to have the answers that I was looking for. And why would they when the road to proper ADHD management and treatment is an oddly controversial one (spoiler alert: the correct answer depends on your kiddo).

To help my daughter, I sought out every new study, every class and seminar, and every possible technique that I could find. I spent a ton of time learning and trying different things to see what worked for my kiddo.

My goal is to gather all of my resources, and I hope to create a comprehensive book that can aid you in helping your young child become a successful and fantastic adult.

Now, a quick disclaimer here, each child is different. As such, one technique may work wonders, and another may not. Your friend may find something that works for them, but it does not affect your child. You might even have two kids under the same roof, and the same technique might have different effects.

ADHD affects each person differently. That's why this happens. The reason someone has ADHD is often that their brain's wires are different than the average person's…but two typical brains won't end up looking the same. By extension, two ADHD brains won't look quite the same either.

Our first chapter dives right into some of these differences. Sometimes the best thing to do is to gain knowledge on the issue before you face it head-on. Are you ready?

Chapter 1

What Is ADHD?

Truthfully, what is ADHD? Why is it so important to understand? Before we dive in, I want to answer that second question for you!

ADHD is, sadly, so fraught with stereotypes that it can be hard to get an accurate picture of what you're dealing with. Many people characterize it in odd, often misleading ways. Maybe it's that children with ADHD gaze out the window and don't pay attention. Perhaps you've heard the stereotype that they can't sit still. There is always the stereotype that they are just badly behaved.

Subsequently, some stereotypes become damaging to people with ADHD. People might say that those with ADHD are dumb when, in fact, ADHD does not affect intelligence. Some of the world's greatest minds are suspected of having had ADHD. When measures such as an IQ test are used, children with ADHD score all over the map, just like children with typical brains do.

Another damaging stereotype that I hope to disprove with this book is that children with ADHD are just kids who need more discipline. Perhaps you've heard this from a judgmental relative or another adult in your child's life. I bring up these stereotypes because you won't be the only one to have heard them. Your kiddo will hear them too, and without the proper understanding, it may lead to the feeling that there is something intrinsically wrong with them when they don't have any control over their condition. Stereotypes like this might follow your child as they step out beyond your house, and with these strategies, you can act as a barrier to negativity.

Now for the question, you came here for!

What Is ADHD?

ADHD stands for attention deficit hyperactivity disorder. It was built upon the former moniker of attention deficit disorder (ADD), which became outdated around 1987. To date, it is one of the most common learning disabilities.

With its symptoms being more understood and some of the stigma starting to lift, more children are getting diagnosed. Today, just under one in ten children are diagnosed with ADHD (Parekh, 2017). Because we still do not know everything about ADHD, and we could still be missing some things, it's likely the numbers are a bit higher. To date, it's more easily identified in boys than in girls. Whether this is an actual gender difference or simply a lack of studies done on ADHD, the female mind is only now starting to be studied (Ellison, 2020).

ADHD is characterized by two main things: trouble paying attention and a tendency not to be able to sit still. As you might imagine, it's first identified when children reach school.

There are many treatments available for ADHD, and I will give a brief list here and give a lot more detail about these in later chapters.

One possible treatment is Cognitive Behavior Therapy (CBT), which is common for many mental disorders and learning disabilities. CBT is the use of specific strategies that focus on thought and behavior, which, in turn, leads to better emotional management. CBT can help with anger and stress management, which will go a long way in helping a child with ADHD.

CBT focuses solely on control of one's actions. This tends to be popular with more disruptive children as it can help them better understand what their behavior is doing and how they can change it.

When your child is diagnosed, you might be (or have been) recommended medications. Medications have varied effects. For some, medicine offers long-term relief, and there might be little to no relief for others.

For help in a child's support systems, there are options for classroom accommodations (Individual Education Plan (IEP), 504 plan, etc.) and opportunities for family therapy.

Finally, for parents, there are training sessions. Much of what we go over in this book are things I learned from attending many, many sessions so that I could help my daughter.

Causes

What exactly is the cause of ADHD? The short answer is that we don't know (yet). ADHD has to do with understanding how the brain is wired. Something that crosses one way in a typical brain will cross differently in the brain of someone who has ADHD. We are not sure what that something might be, although it's likely in the frontal lobe.

What we do know is that genetics can be a predictor of ADHD. As many as 75% of those with ADHD can point to someone else on the family tree who is equally diagnosed or exhibited symptoms.

While we try to study the exact origins of ADHD, we do have some previous work to rely on. Many things can happen to a person that can cause their brain to diverge from the typical path.

A lot of the answers may be in pregnancy. Smoking, drug use, and alcohol use have all contributed to congenital disabilities, including learning disabilities. Now, I am not here to point fingers at all! Many people do not realize they are pregnant, and all of the substances above are addicting. Without a solid reason, they may see no need to stop.

Another in utero impact that can be totally out of our control is stress. If a pregnant person goes through job loss, housing struggles, a pandemic, or any event that causes a lot of stress during the pregnancy, that might impact the baby's development.

Another thing that can cause a brain to diverge from its developmental path is a brain injury. Now, there are some obvious causes of brain injury, like car crashes, for example. However, many other things can cause brain injuries, such as being dropped as a little one or having a lot of concussions as a kid. Any of these may cause altered connectivity in the brain.

Is there an increase in the diagnosis of ADHD? Yes. Does this mean that more kids have ADHD today than thirty or so years ago? Probably not, at least, not this much.

Our criteria is developing, so we are likely identifying children today who wouldn't have been in the 1980s. Adding to that, since we are starting to explore ADHD and its behaviors in girls more, there is a chance that diagnosis could rise to meet boys. There is a chance of overdiagnosis since we still don't know everything there is to know about the disease (this is why a second opinion is often suggested). In short, there isn't something out there that's causing an increase in diverging brains, just a better understanding of symptoms.

The ADHD Brain

What do we know about the brain's role in the creation of ADHD?

We don't know the exact answer, but we have it narrowed down. Currently, testing shows that the difference lies in the frontal lobe (American academy of child and adolescent psychiatry, 2017). It seems smaller and is potentially developing more slowly in children with ADHD. With this comes a chance that neural impulses aren't firing correctly or at a slower rate.

To think of our neural network, think of a telegram service. A message is sent over wires that connect to different parts of the brain and the body to tell those parts what to do. One of these messages comes in the form of the chemical dopamine, which those with ADHD seem to have a deficiency. Dopamine is essentially a motivation chemical. Without it, we wouldn't have any way to get out of bed. People with severe deficiencies can't move. Literally, if there is a fire next to them, without dopamine, the brain isn't sending them a signal telling them to move.

In a normally functioning frontal lobe, we see things like problem-solving abilities, and children develop this naturally as they grow. We also see impulse control, and the little voice in the back of our head telling us not to yell at the person next to us is crucial.

Memory and language are a part of the frontal lobe. Memory is a function we may take for granted. For a child with ADHD, having a memory deficit can make schooling even more frustrating. The frontal lobe also controls our judgment and ability to delay gratification. So are our planning and decision-making abilities. Motivation, the ability to pay attention, and even social behavior seem to be rooted in the frontal lobe. They all require dopamine on some level as well.

Again, we are unsure what is happening but think of your child. How many areas do you think they are struggling within the categories we just mentioned?

The frontal lobe is the center for all of these things (the headquarters, if you will), and dopamine functions as the executor for making these functions happen.

It's hard to see your child act out, get in trouble at school, or do things that you and they know that they should not be doing. While our science hasn't been able to link ADHD to a specific cause, it has shown that ADHD isn't just a behavioral issue but a true brain deficit (one that, I stress, does not impact overall intelligence).

In the future, we are likely to discover a more specific answer as we continue to dig for one. In the meantime, the current research tells us that it isn't just about not paying attention, acting immaturely, or that there is more of a need for discipline. There is a cognitive reason behind everything.

This is the general process of ADHD in the brain for most people, but as I stated before, each person is different, and ADHD may look unique from one child to the next. There are three distinct categories, or types, of ADHD that we will look at next.

Types

I want to introduce you to three children.

Morgan is seven years old, and she's very excited to be going into second grade. Her mother, however, isn't nearly as ready for her daughter to enter this new step. In first grade, the activities were more mobile and fun. Her mother knew that second grade would step it up, and she wasn't sure Morgan was ready. The second grade would mean that Morgan would spend more time sitting still and listening to a teacher and less time with activities.

Morgan's teachers always described her as seeming to be in another world. She always seemed far away and did not pay attention to the lessons. If Morgan were sitting still, she would show signs of apparent boredom. She had a hard time staying on track and keeping her mind on one thing. New information always seemed more challenging for Morgan to grasp than it was for her peers. It was hard to get Morgan's attention, and it often did not seem like she was listening to her teachers. While Morgan never seemed to disrupt class, her teacher found that they constantly had to give her supplies to do her work with because Morgan would misplace hers. Morgan's diagnosis of ADHD wasn't a surprise to her teachers, but it was a surprise to her father, as Morgan was never in trouble or disruptive. She just seemed to be daydreaming most days.

When Morgan's classmate was diagnosed with ADHD two years before she was, no one was surprised. Jamison was a good kid, and even his teachers thought so. However, Jamison's mom always commented, "he just does bad things" in conferences. Jamison was known for being a little immature. While the rest of his classmates seemed capable of sitting still and doing what they were supposed to, Jamison would squirm, no matter what. His teachers asked him if he was uncomfortable, and he always said he was fine. Jamison was also prone to fidgeting with nearby objects. The tape that kept his name tag in place had nearly been ripped off at this point, which annoyed his teacher. Even if Jamison was supposed to be doing his work, his teacher found that he would fidget in his seat or play with little toys that he got from home.

Jamison always seemed to have his eye on the clock and asked when lunch and recess times were more than once each class. Jamison would get up from his seat and walk around the classroom more than any other student. Finally, he rarely raised his hand to answer a question, would talk out of turn, and disrupt others around him.

The last child I want to introduce you to is Eli. Eli was diagnosed with ADHD when he was five years old. Eli rarely paid attention to what his teachers were saying. It often seemed that anything the teacher told him would go in one ear and out the next. Teachers often had trouble getting Eli to complete his work. Eli would often respond that the work was boring when his parents asked about it, so he didn't want to do it. If Eli did his assignments, they would often go missing, and he wouldn't be able to turn them in. When group activities were happening, Eli often seemed as if he wasn't moving as fast as his classmates were.

Eli's teachers noticed that of their students, Eli usually had the most trouble in terms of understanding the information. If they slowed down quite a bit, they were usually able to help, but that made it hard to help other students.

Eli always had a restless air about him. His leg was always bouncing, and he seemed to consistently have something in his hands that he was fiddling with.

Eli often talked to his other classmates, even when the teacher was teaching. An additional worry that his teacher had was that Eli tended to yell at others or at things that were frustrating him, with little thought to the consequences of his actions.

Morgan, Jamison, and Eli have the same diagnosis: ADHD. Nevertheless, it seems to affect each of them in different ways. So far, there have been three identified types of ADHD.

Inattentive

With inattentive ADHD, you are not struggling as much with sitting still, speaking out of turn, or misbehaving. What ADHD is attacking is your attention. With inattentive ADHD, you might miss some of the small things or even obvious things to everyone else.

Distractions come upon you much harder than they might someone else. It's hard to maintain your interest in something, leading to you getting bored quickly.

When you try to focus on a task, you can't. Something seems to get in your way actively, interrupting your focus.

You struggle with having a cohesive thought structure in your brain. Your thoughts are all over the place and hard to get straight.

Learning new things is a strain too, and your brain may struggle to encode this information into your memory.

Daydreaming, or at least the appearance of daydreaming, is a common characteristic of this type of ADHD that can show up in slow movements, not paying attention or listening, and potentially not taking in any new information. Equally, following directions is often a struggle for people with this type of ADHD.

Finally, you are more likely to lose and misplace things. For your kiddo, it might be pencils, paper, missing assignments, etc. For you, it might be things like your phone or your keys.

Inattentive ADHD is often less disruptive to the world, and because of this, it can be easily missed, especially in kids with above-average intelligence.

Let's say, for example, that your child is in kindergarten. They exhibit all of these symptoms. Your child's teacher watches as they seem not to be paying attention, and she is concerned.

But, your child is already aware of most or all of the concepts the teacher is talking about in the classroom. They finish the work quickly and do well. This alleviates the teacher's concerns and keeps the ADHD undetected. That's not to say ADHD can't be detected in children with above-average intelligence or that children diagnosed early with this type of ADHD have below-average intelligence. It shows us that a child's performance may not be an indicator of ADHD.

Can you guess which of the three children above have inattentive ADHD?

The answer is Morgan. Her actions are not disruptive to the environment around her, but they make it very hard for her to learn.

When girls are diagnosed with ADHD, it's often inattentive ADHD, which is harder to spot due to many scenarios like the one above.

Hyperactive-Impulsive ADHD

Hyperactive impulsiveness is often the basis for several stereotypes of ADHD, particularly those where the child acts out and is violent. This stereotype isn't accurate, but it's important to highlight that this type of ADHD is often spotted sooner because the symptoms tend to be more disruptive to everyday classroom activities.

Sitting in one place seems like it would be a nightmare to any child, but it is challenging for those with this type of ADHD. Maybe they are tapping their feet, drumming their fingers, disturbing the others near them, or messing around with a nearby object during a moment when they should be doing something else. They may even get up from their seats when they are not supposed to due to the difficulty they face sitting still for as long as school demands.

People with this type of ADHD tend to be chatterboxes. While there are many people out there who talk a lot, people with this ADHD have a hard time rearing themselves and giving others a chance to speak or knowing when to stop altogether. For example, a student might be trying to engage his classmates in conversation while the teacher is talking. Along with talking to others, you might hear notes that a student with this type of ADHD is good at participating but bad at taking their turn to do so. It's common for them to forego classroom etiquette, such as raising one's hand before giving out the answer. Additionally, they may make loud comments that are not in line with what is going on at that moment.

A person with this type of ADHD may have trouble reading, working on assignments, or participating in other activities requiring a person to be quietly engaged.

Some final notes on this ADHD form are that people with it tend to be impatient, impulsive, and always need to be doing something. Children, in particular, may have trouble waiting for their turn. They might try actions such as cutting in line or pushing other children out of the way. They may be "bouncing in their seat," so to speak. It's also common for children and adults with this type of ADHD to struggle with considering the consequences of their actions. This is a problem not just for those with ADHD but also afflicted by other frontal lobe deficits.

This form of ADHD, as you can see, is more disruptive to the world around them, and it's most common in boys as opposed to girls.

Of the three children above, Jamison has this form of ADHD. He shows hyperactivity, trouble with talking outside of appropriate moments, and difficulty following directions. This stood out very early on in his classroom behavior, and he was able to get a diagnosis and treatment early.

Combined-Type ADHD

People with combined-type ADHD have to fight both inattention and hyperactivity. You can probably already see where this might be going with that name.

Impaired with this type of ADHD, you are likely dealing with symptoms of inattentiveness. You might overlook the small things that everyone else sees. You might have trouble with focus. You might find yourself growing bored within seconds of beginning the task. In addition to this, staying on task might be challenging. Losing everyday items might be a common occurrence. There might be trouble when it comes to listening to instructions. To shorten the list, the attention span of someone with the combined type will suffer.

There will also be symptoms of hyperactive-impulsive ADHD. The trouble with sitting still and the fidgeting that comes with it will be there. There will be trouble with interruptions and talking when one isn't supposed to be.

Eli is our example of a person with a combined type of ADHD. A person doesn't have to have all of the ADHD symptoms in order to be considered as having combined-type ADHD, and they have to have a significant amount that roughly balances the two categories.

I want to highlight that it's highly unlikely that a child intends to be disruptive or not be paying attention or following instructions. It has to do with their brain not processing the proper signals, leading to these outcomes.

Perhaps you may have noticed this already or may not have. The brain is a complex system, and it's not uncommon for one area of the brain to have issues that create more than one problem. Several conditions seem to go hand in hand with ADHD. You may have already seen these diagnosed, be waiting on a diagnosis, suspect it, or your child may only have ADHD. The brain can be quite a spectrum.

Our next chapter will talk about some of these conditions and the emotions your child might be struggling with due to their ADHD. We'll also talk about what might impact school, which has become even more important with education often taking place in the home.

Chapter 2

Conditions Associated With ADHD

ADHD itself can feel like quite the challenge to manage, and for many of us, it isn't the only thing that we will be tackling.

The reason it's essential to understand where ADHD might come from in the brain is because it helps us better understand where some other issues might come into play. The frontal lobe is responsible for a lot, and with an ADHD diagnosis, it is thrown off balance.

Like many of you, I find myself tackling more than one challenge. In addition to ADHD, my daughter has autism. While this book is dedicated to ADHD, I have taken time to learn about both, and I understand that knowing what you can about all diagnoses is essential. With this in mind, I have created a list of some common conditions that come with ADHD to help you better understand how to treat them.

Behavioral Conditions

Few children intend to misbehave, but it is more common in children with ADHD due to the brain imbalance. As we talked about above, each brain can be different, and for some, the chemical signals that the brain sends are so strong that it creates another behavior disorder.

Oppositional Defiant Disorder

Oppositional Defiant Disorder (ODD) commonly starts before the age of eight or after twelve. It is a common behavioral diagnosis that often goes with ADHD.

If your child has ODD, you might notice that they often get angry. They are likely to disobey rules blatantly. If you request something from them, they will likely refuse to help or simply ignore you. If you have other children in the house, they may show resentment towards them. This resentment can also transfer to animals you have or other children they are close to. This can escalate into violence if they experience any flooding, particularly with angry emotions.

They may show signs of being annoyed at small things and make a strong habit of annoying others. It's also prevalent for someone with ODD to blame others for their behavior.

When this happens, especially in younger children, try to walk them through the events. Have them give their version of things that happened. It gives them a chance to explain their point of view and how they think the other person might be at fault. It allows you to point out what they might have done differently to avoid the situation entirely and how it might not be the other person's fault at all.

Every child is occasionally guilty of the behaviors above, but these behaviors will occur much more often for children with ODD.

It's also important to note that children with ODD are less likely to engage in these types of behaviors if they are more comfortable with the people they are with.

Many ADHD techniques that we discuss below will also provide a ton of help for ODD!

Conduct Disorder

Conduct disorder is a disregard for social norms to the extent that it is harmful to others. This doesn't mean shaving one's head, deciding to use different pronouns, or dressing in non-traditional ways. Conduct disorder outlines practices that, at their most serious, involve breaking the law and causing genuine harm to others. People with ADHD often do not think of the consequences they will face when they complete these acts. Instead, what they think of is that there is an adrenaline rush that comes with the action, which can make those with ADHD inclined to try them and prone to this disorder.

Serious violations of home rules can occur, including damaging property, getting angry and breaking out into fights, breaking rules that are vital to be upheld, and occasionally running away.

Most of these actions will not be premeditated, and they are a heat of the moment response to a surge of adrenaline or flooding.

Your child may also engage in acts of bullying and cause fights at school. They may also participate in lawbreaking acts such as stealing, robbery, speeding, and vandalism.

Conduct disorder often does require that a professional step in and help, but there are things that can be done about it.

Continuous accountability is one measure that prevents conduct disorder from becoming something that significantly impacts their life. Laying out consequences beforehand and having a visual aid can help too.

Another thing is allowing the natural consequences to play out. What do you do if your kiddo damages property around the home? Have them pay to fix it. This doesn't have to be a harsh consequence (you can still take a gentle tone), but it does create a cause-and-effect link.

Now, this understandably gets harder if your kiddo broke the law. One thing to remember is that children have their records expunged, so this won't be on their records permanently.

If they break the law, they might be counting on you to bail them out and keep them from facing trouble. Sadly, they have committed an action the court system wants them to answer for, and it's best to learn what can happen when you break the law when you are a child, as opposed to when you are an adult, and the consequences are much more severe.

Learning Disorders

Up next are learning disorders. These are particularly difficult, as having ADHD can already make learning difficult in a typical classroom setting. Below is a set that commonly goes with ADHD.

Dyslexia

Dyslexia affects a person's ability to read. Many have described letters changing shapes (For example, a 'd' turning into a 'b' or an 'm' becoming a 'w.') or the letters seeming to move around the page constantly. This one gets the most attention and representation, and public figures have mentioned struggling with it.

Many schools have programs that can help with dyslexia, and there are several online resources as well.

Dyscalculia

Dyscalculia affects math. Number computation may be easy for someone with a typically developed brain, but that center isn't developing so easily for others.

One important thing to remember is that many careers out there don't involve math. In fact, very few will require high levels of computation. Adults who struggle with math are still very successful.

In the meantime, though, check out those school resources. See what is offered online too!

Dysgraphia

Finally, there is difficulty in writing. Whereas some may have trouble reading, others may have trouble getting the words onto the page.

These have links to a frontal lobe malfunction, and it is possible to have all three. Typically when these issues appear, the best course of action is to create a plan involving the parents, teachers, consulting doctors and psychologists, and the child themselves, especially as they grow older. It does take time and patience, but these issues can often be overcome or compensated for.

Mental Health

Serotonin production is one of the brain chemicals believed to be imbalanced in a way that results in ADHD. The use of serotonin by our brain is widespread, and in addition to controlling the aspects that we see affected by ADHD, serotonin is directly linked to our brain's mental health and wellness. It is currently believed to be primarily involved with the two disorders listed below.

Depression

Depression has been a hot topic. We are seeing a massive increase in diagnoses across the world. It could be that we are better at recognizing it. It could be that we are overdiagnosing now or underdiagnosing in the past. It could be that the current circumstances have led to situations where people are more likely to feel depressed.

Depression, as stated above, is often found in people with ADHD. ADHD can interfere with one's quality of life. Children may feel as though things are not in their control because of their ADHD, including school, behaviors, interactions with others, and others' perceptions of them.

Does nearly every child experience symptoms of depression in their lifetime? Yes, but not at a consistent rate. Diagnostic criteria state that for someone to be diagnosed with clinical depression, they have to experience multiple symptoms of the disease. These symptoms need to be present for at least two weeks and need to have a significant impact on a person's ability to function every day. That being said, there are issues such as minor depressive disorder or high functioning depression, and it's a good idea to keep your eye out for these issues too!

For your child, this won't just be a brief period, and it will impact their ability to function in an entirely different way than ADHD would.

One thing to look out for is a strict sense of misery. That might seem like a lot but think about it. Does your child always seem to be sad or upset? Do they have hope or look forward to things?

This level of sadness and misery will seem so bad that it can make it hard to get out of bed. No matter what you do (Whether it's making their favorite cookie recipe or turning on a favorite show.), nothing seems to make the situation better.

Another core characteristic is that their normal favorite activities no longer interest them. They may engage half-heartedly, or their energy for the activity drains almost as soon as it is gained. Typically, a child with ADHD will focus heavily on activities they enjoy, so this change is very likely to stand out.

Focus and concentration symptoms can be hard to spot since your child faces these every day, but what have you noticed? Has your child seemed off lately? Has there been any sign of their ability to concentrate changing? Perhaps they have suddenly gotten bad grades in what was once their favorite subject. This is another sign of settling depression.

The final sign is a lack, or a devaluing, of their self-worth. Talking with your child about the importance of high self-worth and how they view themselves can act as a preventative measure for depression and help you spot the signs.

Depression is a severe issue. In fact, it can kill. It is best to always keep an eye out for signs in any children. An open dialogue of communication can go a long way. There are many treatment options available, and you should talk to your doctor if you think your child is showing signs, and they can walk you through the various treatment options.

Anxiety

Anxiety's relationship to serotonin is less known, but there is still a documented correlation.

Fear is a normal emotion, and worry is a normal emotion. What is not normal is for it to interfere with a person's daily functioning.

One type of anxiety is known as separation anxiety. Most children show hesitancy when separated from a familiar adult, but children with separation anxiety don't handle it well. They will try to run after the person in question. If that doesn't work, they are likely to resort to methods such as screaming, melting down, or even becoming violent. This behavior will commonly persist for at least a couple of weeks before it's considered to need a diagnosis. Children with separation anxiety are not likely to adjust to their new environment.

They may not engage in other activities and may not even respond to the other adults in the room. Parents can work with teachers and daycare providers, and if it continues to be an ongoing problem, they can talk to the child's doctor.

Another type of anxiety disorder is social anxiety. Social anxiety comes into play with new places and new people. Like separation anxiety, this fear does not just subside. Instead, it gets worse the longer the child is in the situation. There are several ways to combat this. You can try and tour new places when they are not busy or loud, so your child has a better sense of what to expect. You can introduce your children to new people on more comfortable grounds, such as asking to meet one on one with a teacher while you are in the room. With technology, this can become even easier. If strategies like this are not working, talk to your child's doctor about some other things you can try.

Finally, there is general anxiety. This one is often recognized as quite horrendous to those who have to experience it because it is harder to fight. Generalized anxiety does happen to everyone, but it's usually in a manner that is within a person's control. For example, even though you know a school test will be pretty easy and you know that you have studied it, you still experience that feeling of butterflies in your stomach. You are worried that you will fail; the difference is that this sense of failure will leave you after the test. It will not leave someone with generalized anxiety disorder. This constant sense of dread follows them, and they are worried that something terrible will happen even if there is no logical reason to believe it will. To combat generalized anxiety, you often have to dive into cognitive behavioral therapy practices.

Anxiety can place a burden on a mind that is already strained with ADHD. Keep an eye out for signs. Having strategies on hand can make a huge difference.

Physical Health

It is easy to overlook these things until something terrible happens. While it is technically a learning disability, ADHD puts children at a unique risk of physical harm.

Injury Risk

Children with ADHD have an increased risk of injury. Children lack coordination abilities which increases their risk of falling, but those with ADHD have an additional thing to worry about.

Think back to what you have learned about the frontal lobe. One of the things it is responsible for is logical thought. Another thing that it's responsible for is "if-then" thinking. A child without ADHD may logically think, "jumping out the window will hurt me." A child with ADHD, unless they have prior experience to pull from, would think, "jumping out the window looks like fun." The logical fact that they might injure themselves goes missing. With if-then thinking, a child without ADHD may say, "if I run into this busy street, I will likely get hit by a car." A child with ADHD may say, "dad is on the other side of the street, and I want to run to him." As you can imagine, that's likely to cause injury.

There is also the inattentive aspect of ADHD. A child might run through the street without even noticing that cars are on the road.

The hyperactive component is there too. A child might be running around quite a bit on the playground to burn energy, and they are more likely to fall and injure themselves. There is also a chance of developing dangerous and thrill-seeking behaviors in teens. A typical example is speeding.

To combat injury, many experts recommend always wearing proper safety gear, including helmets, knee and elbow pads, seatbelts, and anything else appropriate for the activity at hand. Suppose children engage in activities such as speeding or running into the road. In that case, some recommended steps are for a parent to be firm about the rules and draw up contracted consequences for breaking them (For example, losing the car if they are speeding.).

Staying Healthy

Specific issues may exacerbate ADHD symptoms, or ADHD may increase the risk of particular conditions.

One thing that can make ADHD a lot worse is not getting enough sleep. Our brains use a certain amount of energy and power during the day, and sleeping helps us gain this back and regenerate any neural connections that we might have lost during the day. When we don't get enough sleep, we are not giving our body enough of a chance to replenish that energy. Furthermore, it's not giving our brain a chance to regenerate those connections. Even without ADHD, this can be tough. You might have had the experience of being on autopilot all day or struggling to get through the next task.

As we discussed in the first chapter, people with ADHD are often operating with reduced frontal lobe capacity, where many neurons are attempting to make up some difference. Not getting enough sleep can make ADHD symptoms even worse as the brain hasn't had a chance to repair any neurons.

Another thing that can increase the expression of ADHD is the overuse of electronics. When you've been on your phone for an extended period, do you feel that sluggish feeling? For some reason, your energy is just gone. If you tried to do something now, you would likely run into many mental blocks. This is true for all children too. More and more experts say that time away from the screen is best because it impacts children's behavior. They are less attentive, more likely to misbehave or out of turn, and more likely to refuse or struggle to do things that make them bored. Sound familiar? Children with ADHD are likely to see an increase in these symptoms.

Finally, it's encouraged to have your children eat a balanced diet as a preventative measure. Having a healthy diet increases the outlook for all age groups. In children, it's essential to have as the brain develops, as it can aid in the creation of a healthy brain. This doesn't go both ways (ADHD is highly unlikely to be caused by a poor diet), but having a healthy diet can aid in the development of a healthier brain. Finally, children with ADHD seem to be more likely to develop weight conditions, which a balanced diet can help!

Intensity Of Emotions: Common Causes of "Blowing Up"

ADHD may have a lot of material things associated with it, but one of its most significant issues lies in the behavioral sector. You are probably wondering why your child is so prone to blowing up. Why is it that they experience these behaviors? If you are newer to ADHD parenting, what might you experience?

Flooding

Josh was outside playing with his siblings while his parents talked about his new diagnosis of ADHD. All of a sudden, they heard a cry. When they went outside, Josh was yelling at his younger brother, whom he had pushed. His younger brother was the one they had initially heard, but Josh was also in tears. His face was red as he yelled from being so upset. After a moment, his parents were able to get to the bottom of the situation. Josh's younger brother had been playing with a toy firetruck of Josh's, and he'd broken the ladder. While Josh's younger brother confirmed that he'd broken another toy of Josh's last week, it didn't seem enough to cause this sort of reaction, yet it did.

The reason for this is flooding. With ADHD, the brain doesn't always regulate properly. In this case, the reaction of anger flared up within Josh. For us, that pang might go away after a moment or two, but for someone with ADHD, this response can build and build and build until it becomes an all-out explosion. If your child seems to blow up at small things, this is likely a huge part of why. Working with them on managing extreme emotions can really help!

There is a reverse of this as well. Have you ever tried to use a fire starter, and no matter what you did, it just wouldn't light? The brain has this issue too. Something happens, and the emotional center of the brain signals and signals and signals, and it just… does nothing. The brain may not be able to start an indication of emotion at this point in time.

Criticism

Criticism can feel different to someone with ADHD. Imagine that you are 10-years-old and in an art contest. You finish your work and present it to the judges. "Blending these colors might help you achieve a more real and natural look, but overall it looks amazing!" is the feedback you get. Overall, you see it as positive. They said that your work looks great! That's a win! Someone with ADHD might not see it that way.

Someone with ADHD is in the same contest, and they receive the exact same criticism. Instead of taking the whole message away, they hyper-fixate on the first part. They head to their bench upset, thinking their art wasn't good enough. Even being placed in the top 10 might not be enough.

As they experience constructive critiques in school, activities, or the workplace, they are much more prone to latching onto these things and acting irrationally (Lashing out at the person who gave the critique, for example.) when it was a simple thing or even when the feedback is positive overall. If you are trying to prevent strong reactions, starting with and stressing the positives is often a good way. If you are trying to help them in the future, it might be best to try and help them with listening skills and emotional regulation.

Fear and Anxiety

Have you noticed that your kiddo doesn't want to go places like school or even hang out with others? This behavior can become so intense that they won't leave the house no matter what you do. You're worried about the level of social interaction they are getting (Surely it isn't enough, right?), and you want them to get out more. Yet, trying to get them out of the house has been proven to be a nightmare.

Fears surrounding social situations tend to be worse for someone with ADHD. Making a mistake, acting wrong, or not fitting in seems to be exaggerated, especially with ADHD. We already experience these emotions at a disproportionate level when we are teens, so having this issue can worsen the already crazy situation.

Denial

Anna's family has just been through a difficult time. Their family pet, a cat named Pumpkin, has just passed away. Anna adored Pumpkin and spent time with him every single day. When Pumpkin passed away, Anna's mom did the best she could by preparing a little funeral and giving Anna a chance to say goodbye to her pet. She hoped it would help Anna process, but it didn't seem to be working.

Anna would often come home and put cat food in Pumpkin's dish, then sit by it and do her homework like she used to. When Pumpkin inevitably didn't come, Anna would go outside and call his name until her mom told her she had to come in. Whenever her mom tried to talk to Anna about it, Anna seemed to deny that Pumpkin had even passed away, and she said that he was probably lost somewhere.

Anna's mom was growing concerned. She knew Anna had ADHD, but this didn't seem like a learning disability issue. Instead, it seemed like Anna denied reality.

That's exactly what Anna was doing. Many of us go through a denial phase in order to put off feeling our emotions for "just a little longer." However, with a brain affected by ADHD, flooding is a potential, especially in a situation like Anna's. So, it might be beneficial for her to remain in denial for as long as she can.

This phenomenon can translate to events that cause anger or stress as well.

If the problem persists, try to talk it out. In the case of Anna, her mother might sit down with her and talk about Pumpkin being gone and how it is okay to feel sad or angry. If it continues to be a problem, she might get a school counselor or another mental health professional to help.

Caught In a Storm

When things get intense, we often respond in one of two ways, and we either choose to stand our ground or flee the situation.

Our fight-or-flight response is essential in telling us when danger is around us. For example, if you are camping and see a bear a few feet away, you don't have time to think about the best course of action. So, your fight-or-flight response makes a quick decision. You either fight (or stand your ground and hope you aren't seen as food) or run.

For someone with ADHD, situations that cause even a minor amount of stress can quickly be blown out of proportion due to flooding. The stress emotion doesn't turn off in their brain, telling them that there is a bear next to them when, in reality, it might be a hard homework problem.

Destressing can come in the form of CBT techniques such as running around outside, switching to a different assignment, or taking a break altogether, depending on how strong the reaction is.

Low Self-Esteem

Low self-esteem is not only caused by having ADHD. Society's reaction to the symptoms of ADHD also plays a significant role here.

Storytime! Nia is just entering the sixth grade and going to middle school for the first time. During her last couple of elementary school years, Nia was inside and learning because of the COVID-19 pandemic. She and her parents were able to develop strategies that helped her manage in the face of her ADHD. Thanks to working in an environment that was meeting her needs and a significant amount of hard work, Nia was at the top of her fifth-grade class.

Once she got into sixth grade, things became much more difficult. Her teachers had large class sizes and could not tend to her individually. She was expected to sit for six hours a day with little to no break. Her teachers often forgot that she had a 504 plan and would try to make her understand the same way as other students without trying another tactic. As one might expect, Nia's grades started slipping. Her heart dropped when she got her report card and saw that she had only made 'C's.' She was trying. Why were these grades there? Was she not doing it well enough? Was she not good enough?

In comes the problem of low self-esteem due to something that isn't her fault but the fault of a combination of things (ADHD, stifling environment, etc.).

This is a trap that many children with any setback can get into, and the flooding issue isn't going to make this any easier.

Self-esteem work is essential to anyone, especially in children with ADHD, and it can act to bring them back up after takedowns like the one above happen.

In Nia's case, self-esteem work might look like reminders. Some of the world's most brilliant minds are suspected of having ADHD, and look where they got us. We know that Nia can do it in the right environment, so maybe a switch needs to happen.

Finally, a 'C' is still a passing grade in Nia's case. It may be something to be improved on, but it is enough, which is what matters.

Procrastination

Procrastination is a problem for many of us, but for someone with ADHD, it can be even worse.

Let's say you are faced with a big project, and it is due in a month. You know that there is a lot to do, but you have enough time to do it by accomplishing little each day. Inside your brain, serotonin, our motivation chemical, is being released, and you have what you need to get started.

In someone with ADHD, serotonin is believed to be inhibited. Very little will come when the deadline is a month away. As the deadline gets closer and closer, a little bit more serotonin is released, but not enough for a person to get started. Eventually, the deadline for this massive project gets to be about a week away. There is finally enough serotonin. In fact, a person with ADHD may even experience flooding at this stage. The project still gets done, done well, and turned in on time, but to the rest of the people observing, the person with ADHD looks like they procrastinated.

The example above worked out, but remember, it does not always turn out like that. There is always a chance that the work will not get done on time, something significant will be missed, or the work turned in isn't the best.

Some ways people get around this include using extrinsic motivation (For example: if I finish section X of this report, I will have a good steak dinner tonight.), setting goals and using accountability partners, or pretending that the deadline is earlier than it actually is.

Why Do These Things Happen?

We have talked a lot about how the believed chemical makeup of the ADHD brain contributes to these issues. First of all, many of these things are consistent with an underdeveloped frontal lobe. The frontal lobe is responsible for many things, including things like emotional control, anger management, language, logic, and more. What we expect one kid to grasp may be unattainable to someone with ADHD.

The motivation chemical's lack of serotonin tells us why a child might procrastinate until the last second or why they might not pay attention. It's worth noting the things that are done on impulse that create an adrenaline rush also creates a rush of serotonin, so they are, in a way, motivated to commit thrill-seeking behaviors.

Flooding and a lack of incoming signals can be huge problems. I did include some simple tips for managing these issues, but ADHD is a lifelong condition, and longer-term solutions are often required.

Management Techniques

Okay, so your kiddo has ADHD. This issue comes with an inevitable question: now what? What happens now that you have a diagnosis? There are a lot of semi-long-term solutions and methods that have pros and cons, which we will be going into detail about below.

Medication

Medication is a popular treatment. As the amount of drugs created to treat these conditions increases, so does our prescription of them. Depending on the type of ADHD your child has and how it affects them, you might be prescribed a stimulant or non-stimulant medication. These will act on the issues in the brain and help bridge those gaps.

What are the pros of medication? It can work to make life easier for your child! In many cases, medication has largely solved the issue, and children go on to lead happy lives without the struggle of ADHD so long as they continue to take their meds.

That being said, this isn't the case for everyone. Medication will not work for every brain out there. Furthermore, it's not a one-size-fits-all situation. You may go through a couple of different prescriptions before finding the right one for your child.

Medications also have side effects. They are working in the brain and messing with brain chemicals, which could put a child at risk for mental health issues. The brain also adjusts to having these drugs, so if a child goes off of them after a long period, the symptoms might be worse. Finally, although rare, medication can affect the personality of an individual.

These side effects are things to consider when seeking treatment for your kiddo. They may or may not happen. At the end of the day, the choice of medication is up to you, your kiddo, and your doctor's recommendation.

Cognitive Behavioral Therapy

CBT studies the link between our thoughts, behaviors, and emotions. It recognizes that our emotions are the thing we have the least control over. Instead, they go with the flow of our thoughts and experiences. That being said, we have some control over our thoughts and, generally, a lot of control over our behavior. CBT techniques help you focus on your thoughts and emotions to lead to better outcomes.

For example, let's say that you're driving on the interstate when someone cuts across three lanes of traffic and right in front of you before suddenly slamming on their brakes. You do what's natural; you slam on your breaks, missing their car by inches. The people behind you also come to a dead stop as they try to avoid colliding with both of you and the other vehicles he cut off. Suddenly, he floors it and takes off at a pace way above the speed limit as if he did not nearly cause over a dozen cars to wreck into each other.

What's your initial emotion here? Most people would be understandably pretty upset. Your initial impulse might be to chase him down in a fit of road rage and either honk at him like a maniac or even cause him to crash. At the end of the day, though, what would that accomplish? At the very least, you're going to be held responsible.

Emotions that arise from situations like these can be especially troubling if you have a mental health condition or experience things like flooding. This is where CBT comes in. As you slowly start to move your car again, you notice how you feel, what thoughts you are having, and what behaviors you are experiencing. Then you implement strategies to help with any maladaptive thoughts or behaviors. This might come in handy for children when they are getting angry with someone or getting frustrated in a situation.

There are many techniques out there that your child might benefit from. A counselor or therapist can help direct you in choosing which ones are the best for your kiddo.

Coaching

ADHD impacts our ability to *do* things. Focusing on school, doing homework, household chores, and sometimes even basic self-care tasks can all get neglected in the face of ADHD. Coaching can help in one or more of these aspects. There is plenty that you can do yourself in this arena, but there are professionals who can also help.

A coach looking at self-care and other aspects of life might implement a routine that ensures that they can take care of themselves. They will also work on how to stick to this routine.

Someone may help with the cleaning by assisting them in devising a schedule that they can stick to and teaching them how to master it.

A tutor or a student aide can work with them on strategies for paying attention and being less disruptive in class on the school front. One approach has been to allow a child a fidget toy to focus their extra energy on while in school.

These are all roles that can be filled by you as well!

Talking Through Intensity

There may be things that seem to trigger intense, upsetting emotions for some children. You, and they, might not quite realize what this trigger is, but when they come across it, it leads to a full-blown meltdown.

First of all, help them calm down. No amount of talking is likely to get to them at this moment.

Once you are there, sit down with your kiddo. Ask them to walk you through what made them upset.

This walkthrough process will allow you to make the child aware that some behaviors they displayed were not okay. Since you are not in your child's mind and may not initially realize what went on there, it can also help you connect point 'A' to point 'B.' Finally, as stated above, it can help you identify what might be triggering an outburst. With that knowledge, you can work with your child on coping strategies for these triggers. Or, depending on the severity of the fit, you can help your kiddo avoid them altogether.

Some At-Home Tips

What things can you make a part of your child's routine to help them with everyday management?

Exercise

Children with ADHD seem to be full of boundless energy. Sitting still for long periods is already hard enough for them. Going straight to their study spaces might not be the best idea when they get home. They have already been sitting down for six to eight hours, and that energy has likely curled into a tight ball. Have a set time when they get home where they can get this energy out. If you can, try to encourage some exercise in the morning.

Martial Arts and Other Sports

Healthy activities add to the exercise factor for a kid. Sports involve a lot of running around and hard work, and they also add other benefits that regular exercise does not.

Martial arts, for example, gives them a chance to interact with their peers and a chance to release the frustration that they might have from the day.

Work With Words

Emotions can be shown and felt, but it's hard to understand them without knowing what's happening. One way to help your child with this is to give them the proper language to say how they are feeling, and this gives them a chance to talk through their emotions instead of blowing up.

Clear Boundaries and Rules

Have clear boundaries and rules in place the moment you can. Expectations and boundaries are things that the ADHD brain is good at molding. It also lets your child know what to expect when they come home. When they act out, it is a reference point that is very clear to your child.

Managing With New School Challenges

In late December of 2019, we learned about something that would change the world as we know it for the foreseeable future. Personally, at the time, I didn't realize that COVID-19 was going to be a big deal until about March when things started to look like they were going to shut down. It seemed that we were going about our lives as normal one day, and the next, we were getting prepared to homeschool our children. How did your kid manage with that adjustment?

Many struggled, and for ADHD children, there had to be many maddening aspects. Their routine was disrupted, and there was fear of going outside. Furthermore, all of that was on top of now having to attend school online. Even now, as exposures happen, children must be able to switch and continue their work without a teacher suddenly. How can you help your child with online learning as the world still goes through trouble spots?

What We Can Do

Plan a Schedule

You can let them know what you will be doing next by making a schedule. This schedule helps them have a sense of routine, even if something is going on right now.

Have Breaks

In your schedule, make sure that adequate break time is covered. Let them run around. Maybe try a youtube video or activity, and give them a chance to get up and move.

Timers and Clocks

Along with a written schedule that they can see, having a clock in their line of vision is an excellent step in ensuring that they know what is coming next. Timers can also help by giving them an audible notification of the start or end of a break.

Rewards

Do you ever have those days where you don't want to be productive no matter what is going on? This can feel even worse for someone with ADHD. When other strategies fail, it's okay to let them know those bad days are fine, but we still have to work through them. Extrinsic motivation in the form of rewards (A piece of candy for every page of an essay or 5 five minutes of screen time per lesson or assignment.) can help with these days!

Offer Support

The final part of both this struggle and the struggle of an ADHD child, in general, is to let them know that you are there to help. Offer your support as it's needed. It will help quite a bit in terms of your child's success.

Chapter 3

ADHD and Emotion Control

The first thing Mackenzie's mother notices is that she has woken up in what appears to be a nasty mood. She knows that it's just the ADHD, but she can't help the dread about the potential fight she is about to face.

Mackenzie's mood seems to get worse as time goes on. She goes from appearing grouchy to now being snappy. From snappy, Mackenzie grows to become hostile. When her mom sits her down to do school work, it happens. Mackenzie. Just. Blows. Up. The fit of screaming has Mackenzie red in the face. Both Mackenzie and her mom are shedding tears. She tries to reason with her, but Mackenzie has none of it. It takes about an hour before the outburst seems to be coming to an end. But, the end means that Mackenzie is still sobbing and feeling drained and miserable (After all, blowing up hasn't solved the issue and may have even made it worse.). She isn't stopping because she's no longer frustrated but rather because she doesn't have the energy to continue.

Mackenzie's mother is also feeling several after-effects, including stress, defeat, and some anger of her own. While she understands the concept of flooding, she has no idea what could have sent Mackenzie off in the first place.

This situation can be a reality for many people, and this chapter is designed to help you through it!

The Immediate Steps

We can try everything we know, but the occasional outburst is bound to happen, especially as young children, whether they have ADHD or not, don't yet have a full grasp of their emotions and how to handle them. Some things can be done to help manage and decrease episodes in the long run, but if you're in the position of Mackenzie's mother, what do you do while it's happening? And right afterward?

Time Them and Know

One of the most complex parts of this is that it can feel like an outburst that goes on for hours. You might end up left there feeling frustrated for a while before your kiddo finally calms down.

Start timing their meltdowns and get an idea of how long they last. This is strictly for you, and it gives you something to look at, and as you get an idea of what this looks like, it gives you a general idea of when this will end.

Keep Track Of Strategies That Work

You've probably already tried quite a few strategies for helping them. Some will have worked, and some will have not. That is okay. However, either write down or mentally keep track of the ones that did help. Hold onto these for later use! You never know when you might need it!

Save The Talking for Later

At the moment, your words aren't going to reach them. After Mackenzie finally stopped and sat on the floor crying, She wasn't even aware that her mother had said anything to her during those moments. Many children end up in the same position.

Worse, if those words are said in anger or with an angry tone, children will jump on this and use it as fuel for the fire. Save your words for later, when your kiddo is able to comprehend them. It will help you a lot in the long run!

Get Everyone Calm

When we left Mackenzie, she was still crying. While this might seem like everything is over, in Mackenzie's brain, it isn't. There are still things going on that we aren't quite aware of. Furthermore, Mackenzie's mom is likely to be wound up over this.

Give your kiddo a chance to stop crying and calm down. While they do that, this is the perfect moment for you to calm down and take a few deep breaths.

Help With Emotion Identification

Finally, once everyone is calm, we can start tackling what caused this in the first place. Why did World War Three just happen in your home?

Younger children especially may not yet know what sets them off, just that something did. Walk them through what just happened. Ask them about their emotions in those moments. If they don't know the words, have them describe them to you and see if you can help give them words to use.

Now, first of all, they know the emotions that they are feeling during this process. Second, they've had a chance to walk through what happened. You might be able to figure out what triggered the outburst, and they have a chance to see that their actions weren't the right ones to take.

Discipline In the Face of a Meltdown

Is it your kiddo's fault that their brain isn't wired as well for stressful situations? No. Are they still responsible for their actions? Yes. Is the outside world going to let them blow up whenever they want? No.

Discipline is the way to allow this gap to fill. I want to note that we are talking about directing, learning opportunities, and experiencing consequences that directly relate to their actions. This does not refer to punishment, which is often a physical or psychological thing that does not relate to the issue. Punishment on any child, but especially in children with ADHD, is highly ineffective. Discipline, like the methods below, aims to help teach.

Public Situations

Mackenzie's meltdown took place in the privacy of her own home. That doesn't always happen, especially when you consider that public spaces often have a lot of stimuli that can be overwhelming to a person with ADHD or any disability that involves brain function. A public meltdown can be the absolute worst, but there are effective ways to work through it.

First of all, if you know that your child is likely overwhelmed in a public space, sit down and talk about what it feels like. Help them understand some of the things that happen when they start to get overwhelmed. Let them know that it's okay to come to you and tell you that they need a break. Or, as they get older, let them know it's okay for them to take a break.

If you start noticing signs of a meltdown, try to separate them from the public atmosphere as quickly as possible. Stop the downturn before it happens, if it's possible. If not, pull your child to a safe space, like your car.

Always treat leaving as an option. If your child is having a lot of trouble calming down, it may be best to leave and return to an environment where your child is comfortable. After a meltdown happens, your child will still be feeling many upsetting emotions, and they are also likely to be drained. Going home lets everyone calm down, and it also acts as a form of a natural consequence. It's okay to feel how you're feeling, but it's best to separate from the situation if things become too much.

Avoid Obvious Anger

In the moment of a meltdown, your child will not hear words. If they do catch what you're saying and perceive it to be angry, you might have an even worse problem on your hands.

Anger is something that the ADHD brain treats like a fuse. Once that fuse is lit, there aren't many things that can stop that bomb from going off.

If you can feel your anger start to build up, don't engage. Take a minute to calm yourself down first! Then, try to speak with your kiddo peacefully. Remaining calm, even if they try to escalate the situation, is often the best way to ensure that things are handled in a way that helps a lesson be learned!

Separate

Whether they realize it or not, one standard method used by many parents is to separate the child from the environment. This is essentially a time-out, and while it's mainly used for toddlers, it's great for everyone (including adults).

A time-out will, first of all, separate them from the situation. Your child has had a meltdown or done something they shouldn't have, and it is time to step away.

Next, it gives everyone a chance to calm down. They are upset, and you are upset. A time-out is needed to give everyone a break and a chance to breathe.

Finally, it gives them a chance to reflect on what has just happened.

Once everyone has had their chance to calm down, talking through the circumstance will be received. This includes having them explain their thought process and letting them know that certain behaviors are not okay.

As human beings, we are all prone to and allowed to have our emotions. It's okay for you to be angry, upset, and frustrated.

In these moments, it can be tempting to yell and use punishment methods to deal with the behavior, especially since punishment often has an effect known as instant obedience. In the long run and sometimes in the short run, things will only worsen. It can destroy communication that you have worked hard to build. It can cause your child to try to contain their emotions, which will lead to an explosion later.

Talking through it is much more effective because it gives you and the kiddo a chance to learn and set the boundaries that the behavior isn't acceptable.

Stick To Your Guns

Children with ADHD have brains that do not naturally structure themselves, and they have to rely on their environment to provide this structure for them.

This is another reason why punishment can be a bad idea. Kids with ADHD don't know what to expect next. Instead, having rules in place can make a difference.

It's important to note that your kiddo is likely to resist if you are starting with new strategies. For example, if you, in the past, relied on spanking, and you are now asking your child to walk through what happened and potentially admit where they went wrong, then there is a good chance that they will resist by not staying in time out, or refusing to walk through anything. It can sometimes take several weeks or even a couple of months to solidify in place. When they resist, don't go back to the old method. Tempting as it may be, you left it because it was not helping.

That being said, hold your expectations clear. Every time they get up from a time out or a cool down, set them back down and restart the timer. When they refuse to explain, sit there for as long as is needed.

Strategies For Emotional Balance Through the Day

We would all like to prevent a meltdown or outburst before it happens. Think back to Mackenzie. There were warning signs that she might blow up from the start, and her mom was dreading it. The good news is that deregulation can begin right here, and it doesn't have to wait until someone hits the nuclear button. Some of these strategies are in the moment, and others are things you can add to your everyday routine to bring about a more central sense of peace.

Describing Feelings

Relating emotions gets a mention here as it is so important. We can't control how we feel during the day, only how we react to the things around us. Knowing how we feel and putting that into words plays a considerable part in our ability to control how we act. Start teaching these things to your child. There are many books for kids that focus on learning emotions through stories. After meltdowns, there are also opportunities to give them new words to describe how they feel.

If you notice that your child's day starts similarly to how Mackenzie's did, or you notice a change in mood at any point, pull them aside and ask them to check in and describe what they are feeling. Deregulation and a plan not to let those feelings ruin any fun will be immensely beneficial.

Having A Long Term Plan

Children with ADHD cannot process anger the same way we do and often find that it floods their emotional response abilities. Furthermore, ADHD does correlate with emotional and anger management problems.

This can be an irregular struggle for many, especially if you have a child that blows up quite a lot. Along with this, your child may be becoming a teen who wants more independence but is still suffering from issues due to their ADHD. It may be time to make a long-term plan with your kiddo. The older they are, the more involved they can be.

The first step to most emotional plans is recognizing the emotions you are facing and accepting when it's time to step away! What stepping away might look like can be a part of the plan.

There also needs to be a way to enforce this. There might be a written contract between the parent and the child, and there might be some direct consequences due to an outburst or a behavior issue. Whatever the case is, it is laid out clearly for the child to help them improve.

Meditation

There are many great uses for meditation for a child with ADHD. Meditation is a practice of calm, and you are in a relatively quiet space and focusing on the stimulus you receive.

A typical mediation would involve you sitting down and closing your eyes. You would start breathing deeply and focusing just on that. Once you have confidently concentrated on your breathing, you might do a body scan. Using this, you can find and release tension that's stored in your muscles. Managing a sound and complete scan of your body, start expanding your focus outward. Pay attention to any breeze or AC you might be feeling on your skin. Focus on any smells or sounds around you. You can do this for as long as you like, and then you will slowly come back to your body and then to your breathing.

Meditation helps with things like mental clarity, and it has shown to be a great practice that anyone can benefit from. Of course, children with ADHD might struggle with this at first, and everyone does. Many beginners use music, guided meditations, or a combination of the two.

Guided meditations have an additional benefit because they often have little reminders for when your focus drifts away. You can find these on Spotify, Youtube, or any app based on meditation.

If your child needs some extra help, then try some games. Meditation-based games can act as distractors, and they can help you help your kiddo.

One game is specifically for breathing. Does your child have a favorite toy or stuffed animal? If so, use it for the game. Have your child lay down and place the object on their chest. Have them breathe deeply and watch the movement of the object. Once it seems that they are calm, have them describe it to you.

You can make meditation as a whole into a game by being their guide and using appropriate language for their age. For example, "we sit straight and tall now" and "it's okay to feel squirmy, but I must sit still now."

Walking meditations are also great, but you will absolutely need to be there for this one, as they will close their eyes as they walk. Guide them through meditation as they are walking and help them be in tune with their senses.

Finally, there is a game of freezing in place. If your child is having a hyperactive moment, instruct them to freeze in place. Give them a moment of stillness before asking questions. Draw their attention inward if you can. Ask them about how their body is doing. Does it feel any different right now?

These practices help your kiddo learn to regulate and deal with their emotions in productive ways. Down the line, anyone can use these strategies no matter their age!

Being Gentle With Yourself

Many struggles come with raising a child with ADHD. Some days you will feel fantastic, and on a lot of days, you will sit down and wonder what you did to deserve this.

It's not worth it to bottle up your emotions. You are also a person, and you deserve love and support through the challenges that come your way.

It's normal to feel angry and frustrated, and it's normal to make mistakes. Wanting to yell at your kid when they are acting out is also normal, especially if that's how you were raised. However, knowing that it will make the situation worse makes the burden that much harder.

You have to be gentle with yourself. Just like your child is allowed to feel what they feel, you are too! Take a few pages for yourself. Work through your emotions and acknowledge them. If you need a break, take it. Do what you need to do to get yourself together. If it's several minutes later when you address the situation, that's okay.

Don't be afraid to take the time you need before moving into effective discipline strategies. Our next chapter will get into more depth on discipline and what to keep in mind even after the meltdown has happened.

Chapter 4

Good or Bad Disciplines?

Let us consider the history of discipline for a moment. Well, I'm using the term discipline lightly. Think back to your own experience as a child. Were you spanked? Were the adults angry at you in your life, and sometimes it seemed to be without reason?

These methods were founded on religious-based ideology (For example, "spare the rod, spoil the child."), and it was just the best information we had at the moment until a few decades ago.

Now, we see that this hurts the development of typical children, and in children with conditions like ADHD, it can be especially harmful because their brain isn't processing it in the same manner.

Spanking is a great example because so much research has come about. It harms children psychologically (increased rates of depression and anxiety), can contribute to anger management and violence issues, and interestingly enough, it doesn't work. Children who have been spanked are more likely to repeat the same behavior. While spanking leads to your child listening to you at that moment, a lesson isn't learned (As seen by them being statistically more likely to repeat what they just got in trouble for.).

If you have spanked your child in the past, it doesn't make you a bad parent, especially if you don't have this information.

So, what methods should you use with corporal punishment off the table? You want to relay that some behavior isn't acceptable, but how do you do this in a way that your child can understand. Science has told us that practices like spanking don't work, and it's also clued us into what might help.

Keep in mind a few things. First, every child is different. Your child may respond to some methods but not others, and that's okay. Second, if you are switching to a new approach, there is a good chance your child will resist. We talked about this a little bit in chapter three, but if you think about it, using spanking means your child endures it and then goes back to whatever they are doing. Sitting down to talk takes longer, and they have to participate, admit what they might have done wrong, and plan to fix it. That is not comfortable, especially at first. Plus, with methods like spanking, your child is more likely to be defiant in the long run. It might take a couple of months for the resistance to stop and for you to see fundamental changes. I promise that it will be worth it.

What To Do Before You Use a New Method

It will be essential for you, the parent, to start implementing some things even before you bring it to your child's attention that there will be some new things going on around them. Let's start here.

Your Role

As the parent, you are your child's role model and the person they look to when things aren't going quite right. When you are implementing a new method, it can be more stressful when a child has ADHD. Any inconsistency will be a triggering signal that will take ten times as long to undo as it did to create. Understandably, that might make you feel like you can't make a mistake. You're human, and we are allowed to make mistakes as humans. Still, you can get ready with some strategies to help with this complex issue.

First, work on self-discipline. Train your mind to be calm and patient in these meltdowns. Focus on carrying a sense of calm with you throughout the day, no matter what's happening.

If you feel that things are starting to get to you, it's okay to step out and take a break. Do what you need to do for yourself first. It will help you and your kiddo for you to do so.

Establish a Routine

We've talked about a routine before, and it's getting brought up again in a different light. What happens after a meltdown or a behavior issue? Have a procedure in place for this.

After a meltdown, it can include a cooling-off moment, followed by a talk, and if appropriate, a clearly laid out consequence.

If the conduct continues, behavior issue routines might look like a warning, followed by an initiated consequence.

Consistency like this leaves your child knowing what to expect when they have an outburst or break the rules. It creates a balance that everyone can count on.

Behaviors Outside Your Child's Control

It is very tempting to feel like we need to act on every wrongdoing for our kids to grow up successfully. This isn't the case at all! In fact, it can be damaging to do so.

ADHD comes with a range of behaviors that are genuinely outside your child's control. By reverting to discipline strategies, it can make them feel like a bad kid who can't control that they are "bad." This sense of a lack of control can lead to them stopping effort on good behavior.

The first thing to recognize is that your child makes mistakes and has bad days, much like you. No one in this world is perfect, which is a concept that many people struggle with. Children with ADHD may see being perfect as behaving in a way that makes it so that no one knows they have ADHD. This is unrealistic, as it may be perceived that not having ADHD means that you don't make mistakes. Self-esteem is a common struggle, and being there to reinforce that everyone makes mistakes can be a great buffer.

Another common issue you might run into that is out of your child's control is that of labeling. If you remember, back in chapter two, we talked about Nia. Nia had ADHD and was diagnosed shortly before the pandemic. The two years she spent doing school at home was incredible. They were able to cater to her needs and create a schedule that allowed her to function optimally. She was the highest performer in her fifth-grade class. Then, when she got to sixth grade, she ran into issues. The environment was no longer a strength for her, and at the end of the day, she only received 'C's,' which were passing but not what she was hoping for. As previously accomplished, Nia's capable of getting high marks when her needs are met. When they aren't, she is different.

Your child is very likely to run into similar things, and many teachers are quick to put the blame on the ADHD and add labels like "too slow" or "not likely to succeed." Don't listen to this. First of all, for a teacher to do that is entirely wrong. Second, it's rarely the child. Work with them. Find out what their challenges are. See if there are ways for their needs to be met.

It's important to remember that symptoms of ADHD are not the teacher's fault. Teachers have several children to attend to at any given time, and it can be difficult to pay attention to one kid. Don't assign blame to them or anyone else when the thing in the way is ADHD. When that's our focus, that is the problem we tackle.

Another thing is to distinguish which misbehavior is caused by intention and which are symptoms of ADHD. Imagine, for a moment, that you asked for your kid to help with laundry. They go and grab the laundry, but minutes later, you come out to find the laundry dumped all over the living room and your child staring at the window. This is caused by distraction, which is very common in someone with ADHD. Instead of moving to discipline, as they can't control this behavior, aim for redirection.

In this case, see what distracted your child, acknowledge that it is okay, and then remind them that they have a task to be doing.

A tip from experts is to avoid saying no when you can or to at least give an explanation when you do. When you say no often and with no explanation, any child will be upset. A child with ADHD is going to be impulsive. When you say no without reason, the no isn't enough. They will likely do it anyway and potentially get hurt.

Finally, modeling the behaviors you want to see can help. Your child is looking to you for guidance, and practicing the methods you want them to pick up will have its own effect.

Being a center of calm can help a lot when having ADHD. Modeling Behaviors that you would like to see can help too!

Different Strategies

How do you make discipline stick? What will help your child understand right and wrong without going as far as punishment?

Daily Uplifting Interactions

Imagine that you are a child, and your parents rarely interact with you, except when there is either a significant event or for discipline. You can certainly go for a few days with almost no interaction from this parent. But, what happens when you do something that you shouldn't?

As a child, when this is your relationship with either parent, would you say that you are much less likely to take what they say seriously? You may comply, but more out of fear of losing privileges rather than any understanding of what you did wrong.

Now think about having the opposite relationship with a parent. There is positive interaction every single day, and they make it a point to be involved in all the big and small things.

Children with a parent like this have every opportunity to make themselves seen and heard. Subsequently, children with this type of parent are much more likely to listen to them in the face of discipline.

Most parents exist on a spectrum between these two. Aiming for the latter, even if it is just for 15 minutes each day, can significantly impact the presence of behavioral problems and how discipline is taken.

Careful Direction

It is a busy morning, and as you make breakfast, your child comes over. After greeting them, you give them a few tasks.

"I need you to make your bed, get dressed, feed the cat, and take out the trash." Your child nods and skips off. You come up later to find the bed mostly made and your child half-dressed, wearing pants, a single sock, and still in their pyjama shirt. Their other sock is on their hand as a sock puppet. You don't know whether to laugh or get angry.

As amusing as sock puppets are, it's safe to say that the kiddo got distracted, which is common in people with ADHD.

You listed a few things at once, and they only made it halfway due to their ADHD. A good fix is to put these tasks on a list that they have for reference. This is something that lets them focus on one task at a time!

Pay Attention to the Good Behavior and Let Your Child Know

With children who have typically developing brains, using discipline with bad behavior and letting good behavior happen or simply saying "good job" can suffice.

Children with ADHD need much more reinforcement. When your child has a quality day after a string of bad ones, let them know you see it. When you notice that a task you constantly ask them to do has been completed that day without saying anything, let them know they did a good job and be specific with your words. The ADHD brain creates a feedback loop with positive reinforcement, so this will make them more likely to repeat these behaviors.

Consequences That Are a Result Of Their Actions

We learn a lot when our lack of planning, or something else that is our fault, gets in our way. With ADHD, this can be a strong motivator, and how a lesson ends up sticking. For example, let's say your child refuses to put their coat on in the morning. Let them try going to school without it. When they are inevitably cold, they will remember when it is time to put on their coat the next day.

Using these can help your strategies stick in the long run. Next are just a few extra tips to help round up the chapter!

Extra Tips

These tips come from people who have experience working with kids who have ADHD. Here are some of their recommendations.

Do vs. Don't

We have all seen the typical house rules that use words like "no" and "don't." For an ordinary child, this works okay, but for someone with ADHD, these might be natural impulses and are likely to think, "well, now what?" Instead, make lists of rules that contain "do" statements. Instead of "no running," change it to "walk when you're inside." Instead of "no fighting," change it to "everyone will play nicely together."

Keep a Tally of Behavior

Children with ADHD need things that they can see in order to be able to remember them. An excellent method to help with behavior is to have a reward system in place. Each time a child completes the desired behavior, add something to the chart. You can assign rewards differently (Ex. draw your reward, random rewards, rewards that increase in size the more points they get, etc.).

Keep It Visible

Visibility can apply to many things, including rules, rewards, chores, and a daily routine. Have something visible so that everyone can know what's going on, especially your kiddo!

Show What You Are Asking

Going back to visibility. If you are trying to teach your child new chores or other things, don't just tell them what to do. Your child isn't likely to learn it. Instead, show them. Walkthrough the task and show them what to do each step of the way. When it's your child's turn, let them show you what to do so you can make sure they have the hang of it!

Have A Safe, Cool Down Space

Offering a cool-down space can be for during or after a meltdown or if your child notices that they are starting to get into one and want to calm themselves.

This space should be as separate from the rest of the house as possible. There shouldn't be too much going on in the area in terms of the senses. Put a chair or beanbag and possibly a stuffed toy in this area and make it known that they can come there if they aren't having a good day.

These strategies and tips can go a long way in helping you bring peace to your home, but it's not all about discipline. There are some other things that are highly important to do with ADHD children!

Chapter 5

Burn That Energy With Activities

A huge part of having ADHD seems to be that a ton of energy floods in with the diagnosis. There is a lot to keep track of as your little one seems to bounce off the walls. ADHD is not about sitting still, to say the least. What do you do instead?

All of these activities below are designed to burn energy. There are some indoor and some outdoor options so that no matter what the weather is, you have some tricks up your sleeve.

Dance Parties

Partying down with some dance moves can be great for indoor and outdoor time. You can plan these or have them at any moment that you feel that you need to. Music is very accessible with many of the devices we have today, and if you can get the volume loud enough, you don't even need a speaker. You can have your dance party be an hour-long or a break for one song when you notice your child's concentration on homework dropping.

A Scavenger Hunt

Again, a scavenger hunt can be great outside, but this can also be perfect if you're stuck inside on a rainy day. You can hide anything you want, and this might include stuffed animals, small-dollar tree items, random silverware, leftover easter eggs, or anything else that you have a lot of lying around. The more complicated you make this activity, the more fun they will have with it and the more energy they will burn.

Create A Course With Common Items

Again, a good obstacle course has indoor and outdoor wonders to it. Everyday items such as boxes and cardboard can become anything with little imagination. A giant box can be a car, a boat, a battleship, or whatever you deem fit to make into a game. You can make a lot of cardboard into a maze or a tiny house. Building a fort out of cardboard, pillows, blankets, and more can make this a fun activity that takes energy and makes a great place to quietly spend time when the energy is gone.

Painters tape is something else that you can use, and it won't create any damage. You can use this to create courses (making them follow the line) or build simple boards to use in games like hopscotch or four square. The possibilities with simple items can be endless if we put our minds to them.

Get a Balance Board

Inside and outside are great places to use a balance board. Children with ADHD may lack coordination and other gross motor skills, which can help. A simple balance board will keep them relatively still while expanding a ton of energy. This shouldn't come with much of an injury hazard, but if your child is a fan of quick and sudden movements, try to avoid doing this on hard surfaces (like concrete, for example)!

Playing Ball… With Balloons

This is especially helpful for inside days. Balloons can be made for just about any game, including dodgeball, tennis, volleyball, baseball, and even a game of catch. The perfect thing about this is that most of these options are inside friendly when using a balloon!

Inside Friendly Toys That You Don't Normally Think About

There are certainly some outside toys that should remain outside and some that are rather versatile.

Hula hoops can be used inside so long as there isn't anything breakable nearby. Another example is a jump rope, and both can take up a lot of time as an activity, expand energy, and be perfectly safe inside.

A final example is an exercise ball. This can be used to play on, but if you notice that it's harder for your kiddo to stay during homework or mealtime, switch them to an exercise ball so that they can bounce away and focus better. If you're worried about them falling, exercise ball chairs lock the ball in place and have wheels so you can still move the chair, but there is much less fall risk.

Group Activities

Socialization is important for everyone, and group activities provide the option for everyone to be included. Children with ADHD will especially have a hard time picking up social cues. Activities with friends can be a great way to bridge the gap. You can try sports like soccer, baseball, dance, football, etc. You can also look into active workshops, like swim lessons and day camps during school off times. All of these give your kiddo a chance to get out of the house (which gives you a chance to rest) and make new friends while getting into something they might enjoy.

Solo Sports

Social cue understanding is not the only thing that gets delayed in children due to ADHD. Another thing that I mentioned above was gross motor skills.

Gross motor skills deal with big movements like running, jumping, hand-eye coordination, and balance. Fine motor skills, its counterpart, deal with things like writing, art, and smaller overall movements.

With their gross motor skills falling behind, your kiddo may be more prone to injury from a fall. They might have a reputation for being a little clumsy. In the long run, it's essential to look at some solo activities to help this. And in addition to working on your motor skills, your kiddo will run off a lot of energy. Biking is a great way to do this. So is swimming. A trip to the park that gives them a chance to play on equipment can help too!

Trampoline

Okay, pretty much everyone out there would look at a trampoline and say "yes." They are fun, and you can spend hours jumping away if you wish, and this very springy material is constantly thwarting gravity's effect. You can have games on here or constantly bounce, and the choice is up to you and your kiddo.

On a side note, there are also smaller indoor trampolines that are especially enjoyed by toddlers and young children, which can also provide hours of entertainment.

Knock Out Some Chores

How fun getting some chores done depends on how creative you can get. Outdoor chores, in particular, can be a great way to burn energy.

Gardening can be a great example, especially if your kiddo has a particular interest in the outdoors, plants, or science.

Another example is car washing. Not only is something getting done, but there is lots of fun to be had. And let's be honest, no one is walking away without being completely soaked.

Water Fight

Summer and warm days come around once a year for everyone. During these times, it's nice to cool off somehow, and an impromptu water fight is an excellent way for you, your kiddo, and potentially a few other people, to do so. Get water guns and water balloons, and get whatever you can to make this a fun adventure! Is everyone going to be soaking wet after this? Yes! Will it be worth it? Yes! Everyone involved will have expended a lot of energy!

Yoga

Yoga is excellent for the body, as it gives us a chance to stretch and feel muscles that we might not have entirely realized were there before. Getting your kiddo a yoga mat and some kid-friendly Youtube videos can help them get started with this.

Let it Fly

Don't worry. I'm only talking about paper airplanes. It may seem like such a simple thing as adults, but we all seemed to get so much joy out of making a paper airplane as children. Introduce this idea to your kiddo and watch things fly!

Sculptures

There are so many different ideas when it comes to sculpting!
This engages your child's fine motor skills, creativity, and thought process. The medium is up to you. You can use playdough, modeling clay, kinetic sand, Lego, or whatever else you can find to build with.

Art

Drawing and coloring take energy and are very therapeutic, which is true for painting as well! There are many things here that aren't messy (or are at least easy to clean) that can occupy your kiddo for hours and work on their energy levels.

Take Advantage of Things In Your Community

The biggest example of things to do in your community is attending the library. Go out in public and expend a lot of energy. A library is a great place to go, especially for young kids, because many things in your area can be found there. They often also have kids' groups where your child can take part. Libraries are public but also quiet, so your kiddo is less likely to find themselves overwhelmed.

Other places include parks, community centers, the local YMCA, and more! A quick search can tell you what is nearby.

Concentration Based Activities

Our brains take up a lot of our energy each day. When you work, even if it's a desk job, you probably find yourself tired at the end of the day as you have used a significant portion of your brain.

Children with ADHD often have a hard time sitting still and doing something unless it is of interest. These games are designed to keep them interested, help them develop their brain, and burn a little bit of the excess brain energy we all have.

Sequencing and Matching Games

There are a few options for sequencing and matching games. Memory cards are a simple choice. They can help your kiddo match things, and it also helps with memory. When you turn over a card you have seen before, you must remember where you saw it last. While children with ADHD struggle with memory, games like this can help the brain bridge the gap. There are other, more complex, sequencing board games that kiddos can try as their ability to handle specific difficulties increases.

If you want to increase the difficulty, find a few small objects. Coins or dice are some great examples. Once you have these items, find a piece of cardboard.

Now for the game. Give yourself and your kiddo some of these objects and arrange yours in a row.

For example, if you are using dice, you might put five of them in a row and have them say something like "three, five, four, two, one." Give your kiddo a second to look at it, and then cover the dice with your paper. Have your kiddo make the same pattern and then lift your sheet. If they remembered correctly, congratulate them, and give them a new sequence. Whether you increase the difficulty or not is up to you. If they do not get it right, give them a chance to look it over again before replacing the block and have them try again.

Games such as these are active and one-on-one, so it will be harder for your kiddo to get distracted. They will also serve your kiddo well in the long run by building strength in their memory.

Simon Says

You can get just about everyone involved in some Simon Says. Great for memory, it can be perfect for one's attention span. The child must pay attention to each word to play the game properly. Again, this can help the brain make even more connections.

Puzzles

Puzzles are perfect for teaching problem-solving skills. In order to put together a puzzle, a child has to fit several tiny images together to make a picture. It is not going to get done unless they work on it, so kids are likely to gravitate toward getting it done.

You do not have to make use of jigsaw puzzles to do this. Crosswords, word searches, sudoku, and online platforms can all contain similar challenges that keep your kiddo occupied and using energy for quite some time.

Active Video Games

Things like the Wii or Kinect for Xbox involve body movements in the quest to play games. There are dancing games, sports games, and more! Obviously, these aren't cheap! Many people who play these games post them on Youtube. While it won't keep a score, you can use these videos for motions for your kiddo to mimic. Children of all ages and abilities are often able to occupy themselves for hours using this!

Older Kids

Let's face it; children grow up. There are many activities listed above that an older kiddo in their teen years might reject because they feel like it is for young children. Up next is our list of activities specifically for teens. Here we're going to talk about some new methods and build on the ones we have already discussed.

Martial Arts

Martial art forms may serve teens even more than they benefit children.

ADHD creates loose connections in the brain that can't always handle hormones and chemicals that are there for brain health. Going through puberty floods the system with these very same hormones and chemicals. Martial arts can be aggressive. You can fight in martial arts, and you learn defense. You also literally get to break boards in martial arts using only your strength.

There is an additional benefit that applies more to teens. As your child grows, they are going to want to spend more time outside of the house, by themselves, and with friends. People with ADHD aren't always as aware of their surroundings as others, which can make them an easy target. If your teen has self-defense skills at the ready, you can be assured that they are going to be okay and can protect themself.

Scavenger Hunt: Teen Addition

As a teenager, an in-home scavenger hunt is probably just looking for where they misplaced their phone. However, they might have some fun with them, but not as much as a little one. Luckily, you can make the same concept just a little bigger. Have you ever heard of geocaching? What about letterboxing? Geocaches are hidden in places worldwide, and likely some are very close to you. These might be little pill bottles or whole boxes filled with goodies that you can swap out. There are entire communities dedicated to geocaching.

Much of the same is true with letterboxing. This is very similar to geocaching, but the concept is different. You will need a simple notebook and possibly an ink pad for letterboxing. A letterbox is hidden similarly to a geocache, but inside will be one thing: a stamp and an ink pad (Sometimes these might be dried out, so it can be handy to have your own with you.). These stamps can be letters, numbers, characters, or just something else that happens to be really cool!

Activities like this can be done alone if your teen would like some time to themselves, and they can also be done with friends and as a family. At the end of the day, you will have burnt a lot of energy, which can be an excellent source of fun!

Sports

As kids enter middle and high school, sports become more prominent. There are multiple reasons to get your kiddo involved in sports at the high school age. It has similar benefits for children, but you need to maintain specific grades in high school to stay in sports. This can be hugely incentivizing if your kid has a sport they enjoy.

Building On Art

As a child turning into a teenager, the art your kiddo will likely want to do is going to grow. Painting and drawing may become more complicated, as will other art forms. Let them experiment. It takes a fair bit of energy, and it's building neural connections.

You might try some adult-based coloring books and adult paint by number sheets to foster this. From there, let your teens' creativity come to life.

Making Music

Your child might like singing or marching band or even be in their own small band. Encourage these things; there are many reasons why you should. For starters, music has had reparative effects on many brains. In the case of ADHD, it could foster some amazing developmental steps. It's also another fun way to let out some creativity.

Theater

The art form of the theater still exists in many schools, and where there aren't schools, there are usually other programs. Teens who enjoy being creative can find many things in the theater.

There is, of course, the actual performance side. But, there is also set and costume design, directing, controlling the stage, lighting, singing, and more. In short, there is something in theater for everyone.

Board Games

Our final recommendation is board games (of course). These have been around forever, and they encourage some great things.

The older your kiddo is, the more advanced these games can get. The game of Life, Monopoly, and others can be great for fun and challenging loving teens. You can even look at story-based games. An example of a hardcore story game would be Dungeons & Dragons.

There are many different activities that your child can get invested in to help keep their ADHD at a manageable level. These give a wide range of ideas for all ages to participate. Your child might not love some of them, but they may come to really enjoy others. As we discussed in a previous chapter, take a second to find what works. Then, give that a solid go.

Chapter 6

Nutrition and Well-Being

If you recall, there was a teeny paragraph about health and nutrition several chapters ago. That paragraph does not do justice to the issue. Diet is of vital importance to everyone. In America especially, the laws on what preservatives and additives can be added to food are pretty lax. So long as it will not immediately poison a person, you can pretty much get away with it. Because of this, we have to be especially careful of what we are adding.

Let's visit two children in the fifth grade. Both have ADHD-combined types.

Esme gets up and has eggs and berries for breakfast. Her mother packs her lunch and sends her to school.

Cameron wakes up and eats some toaster waffles for breakfast. His mother has also packed his lunch before he goes to school.

Both Esme and Cameron sit in class. While Esme is constantly fidgeting with a little cube that she has on her desk, at the very least, she seems to be paying attention and getting her work done.

On the other hand, Cameron is bouncing up and down in his seat. He keeps staring at windows, other students, and anywhere else that isn't the whiteboard he is supposed to be looking at. It bugs his teacher to no end, but she tries to be patient, knowing that it isn't his fault.

Both children eat lunch. Amy's lunch contains some leftover whole wheat pasta from the other night and some chicken and vegetables. She gets a Gatorade as well, and Cameron takes a Lunchable as well as an apple and a juice box.

During recess, both kids are running around like crazy. After all, they have been sitting inside all day. However, as they line up to go back inside, Esme seems worn out but alert. On the other hand, Cameron has an exhausted look on his face. He keeps trying not to fall asleep in class, and he crashes about an hour later. The teacher wakes him up but lets it go when he falls asleep a second time. Both are picked up, and as they go home, both have the same energy levels again.

Despite the same diagnosis, you can see how they behaved differently throughout the day. This is a common pattern with everyone. Let's take a look a little further into this.

The Why and the How

Why did Cameron seem so different? To be honest, when a typical child is given a lot of processed foods in a day, they will struggle. Again, it's challenging to do something about this in some countries because preservatives seem to be in everything. I promise though that it is worth the effort. Some foods seem to positively impact brainpower, leading us to believe that they can help with ADHD.

This does beg the question, "how do I get my child to eat it?"

Cameron's mom knows that he is a picky eater. Along with this, she has to consider the fact that she works, so she cannot make a meal from scratch every day. Many moms and dads are in the same position, and I feel you on this!

One way to help your child has to do with the power of natural consequences. Remember a few chapters ago, we looked at a little one who didn't want to put their coat on. Rather than battling them about it, the parents let them go without it. The child did find herself cold throughout the day and learned the importance of wearing her coat. A similar effect can be taught with the food that we consume.

When your child refuses to consume food that is better for them, in favor of consuming highly processed food, let it happen at least for a full day. When their energy levels deplete and they have a more challenging time with day-to-day tasks, help them connect to the fact that the food causes this. When they have a better diet day, mention how great it is that they can focus so well and that it must be because they ate so well. Making this distinction will help your child naturally understand how their diet influences their energy levels.

Meal prep is another thing that parents can do for themselves if they find that they are swamped throughout the week (as many of us are). This doesn't have to be super complicated. You can make a giant batch of a single meal or a few medium-sized batches of meals that everyone likes and pull from that through the week. Alternatively, divide it into containers right at the beginning; the choice is yours.

For kids that absolutely refuse and are generally picky eaters, you can knock many healthy things back into them by making them yourself. You can make homemade pizzas, chicken tenders, and other common foods at home with ingredients you can find pretty much anywhere. It also gives you an idea of what your kiddo is actually consuming.

Finally, involve your kiddos in the process, especially if they are older. If your child is a teen, you can have them choose the ingredients at the store and make their lunch, with help as needed. For younger kiddos, they can also assist in making lunches and helping you prepare some of the meals listed above.

Many kids, especially those whose brains are wired a bit differently, prefer foods that taste good and are familiar, and this especially pertains to junk foods. It often takes several different strategies to teach kids about foods that are generally better for them. It's absolutely worth it, though!

MyPlate

Let's start with this question: what does healthy food look like? Today, diet culture sends messages about good and bad foods and tells you what you should eat. Many diet plans out there focus on telling you exactly what to eat and eliminating certain food groups, which will not help you and will not help your kiddo.

The vast majority of certified people in diet and health sciences all refer back to one thing: MyPlate. MyPlate is the American government's research diet system. It does not eliminate anything, but it focuses on what foods are better for you and what you should put more focus on eating. MyPlate isn't the only existing database like this. Many countries have their own versions based on a healthy diet and take into account the food produced in that area.

If you're looking for some information specific to your kiddo, you might find some help through the MyPlate website or the website specific to your region.

Foods To Focus On

Your child's diet does not have to contain healthy foods solely, but as you create meals for your little ones, these are the best things to have the most focus on.

Complex Carbs

Here is the first one! Now, many diet programs say that carbs are a terrible food and you should cut them out; don't do that! Carbohydrates are what our bodies thrive on, and while some carbs are a sugar load, others are not. As you might imagine, complex carbs fall into the latter category.

Carbs (both complex carbs and simple carbs) are energy units. How much energy something will give you is determined by how many carbs it contains.

Complex carbs are called complex because the body genuinely takes longer to break them down. This means that there will be a constant fuel source in your body, and you will experience a consistent stream of energy as you go about your day. You will have better energy levels, feel full for a more extended period of time, and have a longer chance to use the energy you put into your body.

Now, let's talk about what contains complex carbs.

The first thing is anything labeled "whole grain." When you buy bread, noodles, rice, and anything that happens to be a carb and bread-based product, look for that whole grain label. Often, this means that a simple substitution might be needed, but it will do the trick! This includes cereal too. Some cereals are based on simple carbs (which we will talk about in a minute), whereas some are based on complex carbs. Whole grain will be your key to discovering which is which!

Next is any sort of legume. These are a great source of protein as well as energy. Legumes are commonly known as beans. Now, certain beans aren't necessarily legumes. They are simple carbs that won't provide the same benefits. The bean types you can benefit from are listed below:

- Black beans
- Lima beans
- Soybeans
- Cranberry beans
- Pinto beans
- Lentils
- Red kidney beans
- Fava beans
- Garbanzo
- Yellow and green split peas
- Black-eyed peas
- Great northern beans
- Cannellini beans
- Mung beans
- Adzuki beans

There are plenty to choose from, as you can see. Many grocery stores will sell mixed beans by the bag.

Yet another excellent example of complex carbs is fruit. Fruit is a fantastic energy source, and as an added bonus, it's sweet, so you can easily convince your kiddo to have some.

Finally, starchy vegetables are complex carbohydrates, and your kiddo will probably enjoy these too. Starchy vegetables are usually root vegetables, and they include regular and sweet potatoes, beets, turnips, corn, carrots, and squash.

Lean Meats and Protein

Protein is essential to the body. From a young age, doctors stress the importance of protein in a child's diet. I've heard the phrase "you need to eat your protein to grow big and strong" multiple times, and it's true! Protein is actually essential for muscle growth. It also helps with the regeneration and building of cells within the body. Have you ever heard that your body cells are completely regenerated every seven years, and you are an entirely new person? Science has yet to back up this theory, but many acknowledge that this may be true, given that this process does occur (we just don't know at what rate). Finally, protein aids in enzyme and healthy bacteria production in the body. In short, it runs several essential functions that we need in order for our bodies to work correctly.

Lean proteins are generally better for you. At the same time, non-lean proteins (which tend to have more fat) are not harmful to you in small quantities. However, when they are consumed regularly over long periods, they can cause some issues, such as heart attacks, heart disease, strokes, high blood pressure, and diabetes. The proteins to keep limited include red meats such as beef, pork, lamb, and to a lesser extent, eggs.

Now, lean proteins include white meats such as chicken, turkey, and other bird-based meats, and it also includes fish and shellfish of all kinds. Tofu is a good source of lean protein, and so are legumes. Low-fat dairy like 2% milk, low-fat yogurts, cottage cheese, etc., and nuts are also on this list.

These foods will help your child's body keep up with their activity.

Fats (Well, Healthy Fats)

Much like our carbs, there are two types of fats you should keep your eye on. One is Saturated fat, and the other is unsaturated fat. Saturated fat is the bad one. Due to a series of processing that removes a lot of vitamins and minerals, it essentially adds weight to the poor person who is trying to enjoy their meal.

Baked and fried foods contain saturated fat, and processed meats contain saturated fat. Whole fat dairy (whole milk, whole yogurt, etc.) and solid cooking oils (packaged oils) contain this fat.

Now for the fun list! Unsaturated fat looks quite different, and it hasn't been over-processed, so it still has the essential things that children need. Fat helps the body break down the vitamins from food and supplements and puts them where it needs to go. The vitamins it concentrates on include vitamin A, vitamin D, vitamin E, and vitamin K.

Omega-3s are the fats to be on the lookout for. Due to their high demand, any foods that have been enriched with this fat are going to advertise it.

One common food that contains omega-3 includes fatty fish, and this is typically tuna and salmon. Another example is tree nuts (almonds, walnuts, hazelnuts, etc.). Avocados have been recently discovered to contain a good balance of fat, and you can find them anywhere. Finally, there are seeds, and Chia seeds, flax seeds, and pumpkin seeds are great examples that can help add healthy fats to your child's diet.

Vitamins and Minerals

While essential to every child's growth, children with ADHD further benefit from the regular inclusion of vitamins in their diet.

A very recent study shows that vitamins (referred to as micronutrients) stand a chance of improving symptoms of inattentive ADHD. This includes benefits for combined-type, and it can also help those with the hyperactive-impulsive type.

Along with this, there is something to keep an eye out for. Children with ADHD seem to run into trouble meeting their needs for iron and zinc levels.

The best protection against this is first to make sure your kiddo is taking their vitamins each day, and second, ensure that the vitamins they are taking include these things. Some other vitamins and minerals to be on the lookout for include vitamin B6, vitamin D, calcium, and magnesium. Along with making sure that they are taking their vitamins, you can double-check that they eat several different foods over the course of the day. Many vitamins naturally occur in food, so variety can increase your chances of getting it into your diet. Some foods to focus on have been on our lists above, including fruit, vegetables, whole grains, low-fat dairy, seeds and nuts, and fish.

Your kiddo, overall, should have a well-balanced diet. Doing so may not cure ADHD, but it can seriously help mitigate the symptoms.

Our bodies can only function at the rate they are fueled. This tends to hold true, no matter what age a person might be. When we add conditions like ADHD into the mix, the body might be trying to work overtime to make those brain connections. Not only will these foods help keep your child going, but a general regimen of eating right improves overall brain function and helps create more brain connections. At the very least, it will make things easier for your child.

With that being said, some foods will make ADHD symptoms worse (either slightly or by a lot). Next, we will discuss what those foods are and why they do what they do.

Foods That Your Child Should Avoid

Now we will cover things that are either bad for the developing body or seem to have an effect on ADHD symptoms. You don't necessarily have to cut these foods out of your diet, but it is highly recommended to limit them as much as possible.

Artificial Coloring

I'll admit, I was a bit surprised by this one. Artificial dyes and food colorings are very popular in America, arguably more so than in other countries. Accentuated color seems appealing until you realize that it's either heavily regulated or banned in many regions. This is because they don't really add to food and do a bit of unnecessary harm to the individual who consumes them.

These dyes are created by chemicals and can trigger hyperactivity and other ADHD symptoms.

Most candies (excluding some chocolates) are made with artificial dyes. But a wide range of other foods is too. Chips, dips and spreads, juices, bottled tea, and sometimes even items like bread or fries can contain dyes.

Do be on the lookout. Most ingredient lists won't say "artificial coloring" on the label, especially with the recent discoveries of how harmful these dyes are. Instead, they might say things like RED 40, YELLOW 6 (a popular one that is banned in Norway and Austria), BLUE 10, etc. Lookup any specific colors you see, as some are more harmful than others. Some might do relatively minor damage to you, while others are bad enough to be banned in some countries.

Your child does not have to forgo these dyes entirely. If it's a lovely weekend summer day and everyone's getting some fruit punch at the park, that's one thing. However, if it's right before a school day, that is another story.

Refined Sugars and Simple Carbohydrates

I have grouped refined sugar and simple carbs together because there is a lot of overlap in the food that contains them.

Again, refined sugar is very heavily processed, and it can do a lot of damage if consumed continuously over time.

Both refined sugar and simple carbohydrates have a lot of the same effects that red meat does, including leading to heart disease and attacks, strokes, type 2 diabetes, high blood pressure, and more. The difference, though, is that red meat still has protein benefits. Refined sugars and simple carbs do not, and these are processed so that everything beneficial about them is stripped away, except for the components that contain energy.

In refined sugars, these sugars and energies are running rampant through your child's system, making them hyper and giving them that sugar high.

The same is accurate for simple carbs, and it doesn't have the slow release that complex carbs do. It gives you energy and does it fast, but it takes it away as soon as your body has digested it. To make matters worse, when your body digests it quickly, any energy not used is stored as fat.

Refined sugars are often found in typical unhealthy foods like candies, snacks and chips, and bakery items.

You can find simple carbs in flour (white flour), white bread, white rice, regular noodles, as well as many other things out there. Whole wheat items are the ones that haven't been stripped and processed, which is why these are great labels to look for.

Again, these don't necessarily have to be cut out of a diet altogether, but it is best to limit them.

Caffeine

Caffeine can be especially hard if you have a teen on your hands.

ADHD is naturally something that messes with energy levels, meaning that they can sometimes be very high. Combining the two may get you a rocket ball of energy.

Another thing not to mess with is mixing caffeine with medication (at least without talking to a doctor). Many medications prescribed for ADHD are stimulants, and caffeine is also a stimulant. Combining the two can create quite a hyperactive person. It can also be dangerous, and it may cause severe anxiety and induce an anxiety or panic attack. Caffeine is also known to have adverse effects on the body when you drink a lot of it, and it can commonly affect the heart and your nervous system. Finally, it can cause a loss of appetite and insomnia (which is also a risk with medication).

Caffeine is harmless to the average person if they are not drinking a crazy amount. But in someone with ADHD, especially if they are taking medication, it can cause the body to go haywire.

Caffeine is not just in coffee either, and you can also find it in teas, sodas, some juices, and even things like chocolate.

Sample Diet and Best Tips

There are, of course, some tips that should be shared that can help you manage food intake and ADHD to lead to better symptoms. I want to share these with you, and I want to share a diet plan that is generally already catered to many of these tips.

Be On the Lookout For Sensitivities and Allergies

Children with ADHD seem more prone to having food sensitivities and allergies. Severe allergies are easy to spot and should be avoided at all costs, but some allergy symptoms are mild. Hives, if they are underclothes, are one example. Other things to watch for would be your child complaining about their mouth hurting or feeling numb, and this is a sign that they might be developing an allergy.

In a comparative example, a friend noticed this happen with cinnamon one year. She largely ignored when her mouth would go numb until she experienced an anaphylactic shock. It is scary to think about, but this can happen.

There are foods that cause sensitivities as well. If your child complains about an itchy mouth or an upset stomach, that is a sign of sensitivity. Your child's body may also reject the food through vomiting or diarrhea. Keep track of what foods cause this and see if you find a pattern. Given that it's more common in children with ADHD, it's something to be cautious about!

Balance and Routine

A healthy routine and balance have proven to be effective in helping those who have ADHD.

Having three balanced meals in a row, with a snack or two spaced in between, has proven effective in all age groups and with typical and atypical children.

Try to include at least two to three foods from the list above at each meal. Add fruit and whole grains at breakfast. Add protein and vegetables to their lunch, and the list goes on.

Another popular tip is to have a schedule for eating that your kiddo can stick to. It will help your kiddo out with the expectations, and routine always tends to help manage ADHD. Finally, skipping meals is not a good idea for children with ADHD. Children with ADHD tend to be very active, so skipping meals might lead to low blood sugar. If your child has easy access to snacks, it might be tempting to overcompensate their loss by snacking on junk food, which will likely lead to a very hyper child.

Have Things Prepared In Advance

We talked about meal prepping a little at the beginning of the chapter, and I will stress again that it can be helpful to maintain healthy eating. Another thing that can help you is preparing some healthy snacks and having them in easy grab reach. These can include fruits like apples, grapes, oranges, or strawberries, including vegetables like carrots, tomatoes, celery, or broccoli. Nuts are another excellent option, and having some whole wheat bread with a nut spread (peanut butter, almond butter, or hazelnut spread) is a great idea too. If your child is craving something sweeter or richer, these spreads can help with that too!

Children with ADHD tend to be constant balls of energy! Having things ready from the go is a little step to help you keep up!

Eliminate Slowly

We have talked about many different foods that might contribute to worsening ADHD symptoms. It may be tempting to remove all of these from your kiddo's diet immediately and get them started on healthier options. Here's the thing, though: your kiddo is used to these foods, and so is their body. Making such a sudden switch is likely to send them into a rage and send their body into a shock before it balances itself out again.

Try eliminating things one by one. Either make a plan or if your kiddo is old enough to understand the nuances of eating right, sit down and talk with them. Let them know why you think this will be a great idea. Let them know that you think this will be good for their

ADHD and list all the benefits. Eliminate one food a week, and if your kiddo is old enough, let them make the schedule to give them an aspect of control.

Restriction

The restriction is for those kiddos who may have a lot of allergies or you suspect that other foods are affecting their ADHD.

I will add here that it is possible that certain foods that don't affect ADHD expression in other children do affect it in your children. This isn't highly researched, but each body is different, so this is an excellent way to test your theory if you suspect something.

With this idea, you cut their diet down to very basic foods. These are going to be hypoallergenic foods that won't cause any sort of thing in the body.

Stay with this for a few weeks (a month at most), and then start reintroducing some foods. Only introduce about one to two at a time so that if the body or brain experiences a decrease in function or there is an adverse reaction, you know the cause. Several diet guidelines out there can guide you on the minimum amount of foods needed to ensure that your child is satisfied both in terms of hunger and nutrition needs.

It is worth noting that this plan is best for older kids. For young children who don't quite understand everything about allergies and food sensitivities, this diet means potentially getting rid of foods they love, which is a great way to induce a meltdown.

Older children can keep track of what's going on in their bodies. Have them keep a log and track any changes (even embarrassing ones) that happen in their body so that you both can get an idea of what might be causing problems.

The only warning I can give for this tip is that it's going to be a process, and it should only be undertaken if you have concerns about how food might be affecting your child. If you have these concerns, this is a great way to put them to the test and find out what is going on!

Diet Idea: Mediterranean Eating Pattern

The Mediterranean diet is one that is always on the popular diet list, but it's never near the top. That's because it's not created by someone who intends to make money from it and, therefore, has little marketing power. That being said, it has proven beneficial to those who follow it.

The Mediterranean diet is based on the culture and food choices of those around the Mediterranean Sea. These cover people in regions of Spain, Greece, Italy, and Portugal.

Because of the sea, their primary source of food is fish and small game, and their land is rich enough not to need processing to increase the quantity of food they grow.

This diet includes every food I have listed above and appropriate limits for the food that can hurt those with ADHD. If you are looking for a guideline of how often your child should be consuming certain foods, the food pyramids built off this diet can help!

It was insane for me to learn how much food and a person's diet choices can affect the brain, and it was even crazier to understand that some foods actually could harm my kiddo.

Luckily, with the correct information, you can balance things out. With everything in effect to help manage ADHD, it can grow into something beautiful. You do not always need to feel like you are fighting ADHD, which we will discuss next.

Chapter 7

ADHD Is a Superpower

Why is having ADHD viewed as such a horrible diagnosis? It seems that there are many people out there who see such a thing as something that talks about the very character of a young child. It is such a powerful label, yet it doesn't do much to describe your child at all. People with ADHD are brilliant. They are a powerhouse and a force to be reckoned with. Some of the greatest minds are thought to have had ADHD.

Today our world is designed and structured around the ability to sit still and work for long periods. Typical individuals shouldn't even be doing that, and frankly, the ADHD brain isn't designed for that, and it's designed for activity, action, and creativity.

There are several benefits to having ADHD. Many people with the diagnosis have said that they don't mind having it, and there are several famous names out there that have come out and said that they have ADHD.

In this chapter, I want to take some time to talk about the benefits of ADHD. They aren't talked about enough, and opening this discussion can help many people out there see how ADHD can lead to huge benefits.

Finally, I want to give you some examples of individuals we've all heard of who have ADHD. As your child grows, they might struggle. They might listen to negative messages telling them they aren't good enough or won't be successful. Let's see some real people that prove this wrong. I can help restore some faith.

Benefits

Hyperfocus

Have you ever seen someone with ADHD enter hyperfocus mode? Because it is incredible!

Hyperfocus is an incredible state where everything else in the world fades into the background. It is just you and the thing you are working on. The end result is work that is not only complete but of high quality. Hyper-focusing can help some people with ADHD get away with procrastination while they are in school. But once they leave the education institution and are doing something they love, they have a real chance to do something unique with their hyper-focusing skills.

Engaging hyperfocus involves key elements. A looming deadline can absolutely engage hyperfocus, but how close to the deadline depends on how interesting the task is. Speaking of which, another thing that can engage hyperfocus is an exciting task. For some out there, it does not matter how big or complicated the task is; if they are interested, then the job will get done in just a moment.

Hyperfocus cannot be engaged on demand, although it would be cool if it could be. That being said, many professionals out there have a few strategies that help them lock it in. These strategies are specific to how their brains work and help them get things done! Can you think of any strategy that might have worked for your kiddo in the past?

Resilience

Think about this. Your child is facing many problems each day as a result of having ADHD. In order to move past these obstacles, children have to engage in problem-solving techniques and ideas, which naturally lead to better problem-solving skills down the line.

This is also true for building resilience. Children with ADHD do not have an easy world to face, but they do it every day. Even teachers in public schools note that children who have ADHD tend to be more resilient than others.

Such resiliency and problem-solving skills can take them so far in life. Many jobs look for these skills. Owning your own business or being an inventor requires such prowess. I am not here to glamourize the process of getting them, but at the finish line, there are many amazing things to be said about these skills.

Creative and Outside-the-Box Thinking

Here is another area where ADHD kids excel. You've probably seen this yourself with your little one.

Children with ADHD tend to be more creative. This does show up in art forms, but it is also present in their ways of thinking about the world.

Creativity is a beautiful trait to have. It brings so much more to the world, and it allows your child a chance to build things and give something to the world while having something to share with others.

The same is very true for those who wish to think outside of the box. The world has too many people who can't do so. So many people look to outside-the-box thinkers to solve problems.

Again, both creativity and problem-solving go a long way in terms of being an adult and making money for yourself. Imagine what they can do later if your kiddo can develop these skills.

Conversationalist

Here is my next question for you! Have you ever had a conversation with an adult with ADHD? You probably have, but how in-depth did it go?

People with ADHD, especially adults with ADHD, know how to have a great conversation. This doesn't just mean that they can talk. They know how to make a conversation interesting, they know how to make it cover every topic under the sun, and they know how to keep you entertained and engaged.

Furthermore, people with ADHD have shown in studies to be able to pick up on the moods of others at an easier rate than those without. This means that they can read the room first, and going into a sudden situation is something they can pick up on. They may also be able to sit with someone looking to buy something from them and be able to read the person pretty well.

Again, when it comes to the adult world, the possibilities with these skills are endless.

Spontaneous Ideas

In childhood, it is called impulsivity. It's sadly fair to do this, as young children don't quite know that they are vulnerable to injury, and they tend to do things that might get them injured.

As an adult, though, we tend to have a grasp on the fact that jumping off a building to fly is a bad idea.

For typical adults, this perception gets even more narrow. That means that we might be less likely to diverge off the path or try new things. That's not always true for someone with ADHD. They are likely to try new things. This might mean they try sushi, skydiving, or meeting with a new client, and when they realize their current strategy isn't working, they change it up.

These aren't just great for one's career, but spontaneous ideas also bring about a great deal of life satisfaction.

Consistent Energy

People with ADHD can keep up with the busy world! Whereas a typical individual might struggle, someone with ADHD can be energized at most moments.

Again, this isn't just great for the working world, but imagine doing your job all day and still coming home giddy with energy to do something that you are excited about. It's exhilarating to think about, isn't it?

ADHD will sometimes look like struggling in this crazy world where so many crazy things are happening at once that you don't know what to do. It might sometimes look like getting overwhelmed and burnt out. It sometimes feels like there is so much going on in your head at once, and you don't know how to stop it, yet if it doesn't stop soon, you are going to scream.

It can also look like someone who has suddenly hunkered down to produce fantastic work. It can look like someone who is creative and thinks outside the box. It's breaking down social walls and keeping everything together and entertained. ADHD is so many things wrapped into one package.

I understand that you and your kiddo are probably struggling a bit, and I offer this to show you that ADHD isn't the end. There are many great things about it, and next, we are going to talk about how to leverage these abilities.

How to Make the Most Out of This

Top Tips

Many of the skills mentioned will serve them well in adulthood, so long as they know how to use them! Here are some ways to practice early!

Hyperfocus can become an early practice. Help your child find some of their big interests. Foster them and give them time and space to work on these interests. The results of this might surprise you!

Resilience will foster itself naturally, but having low self-esteem can hinder this. If you start to notice that your child's self-esteem is dropping, try doing some self-esteem work to bring it back up. When they face challenging situations and cope well, it can build resilience. If they do not manage well, or something in their coping strategy fails, it can lead to low self-esteem. Should their coping strategy fail, a great way to build resilience and prevent a self-esteem plummet is to sit down with them and make a plan for next time. Think about what can be done differently. Is there a new strategy to try? This preparation has them ready for next time rather than thinking they cannot handle something.

Creativity can be fostered in much the same way that hyperfocus can. Give them space, materials, and time, and let them explore their interests. The more opportunity we have to use our brains for creativity, the more it will foster and develop.

Look into opportunities your child can jump into for those conversational skills. As children enter high school, there will be opportunities like student government, debate, the newspaper, and more! These are great places for those conversational skills to be put to the test. With supervision, you also might let your child give social media a try if they are interested.

As children share their spontaneous ideas with you, consider them. Try not to say no too quickly when your kiddo shares a vision. Let them entertain their new ideas.

People with ADHD can grow up to be unique and talented human beings. It's going to be interesting to see what they might do next!

Management Ideas

How do you keep ADHD in check with the aforementioned abilities? How do you let them flourish but still restrain yourself enough so that you don't blow people away?

First things first! Have a to-do list, a planner, or something that will help them keep track. I know I've mentioned it before, and it's such a common tip, but trust me, it really helps! It gives them a visual reminder and helps them know what to do next and plan out their day.

The next suggestion is to time tasks. If you have ten things to get done today, you don't have time to hyperfocus on one of them and do it perfectly. That's where time limits come in. Setting a timer on your phone can help you know that it's time to switch to another task.

ADHD superpowers enable great success when kiddos know how to leverage them properly!

Celebrities

Children always need positive role models in their lives. This is something that a child can look up to. A role model is someone that they want to be like. Many celebrities and professionals have talked about having ADHD. Here are a few you should let your kiddo know about. Give your kid a chance to find someone whom they might see as like them that they can admire.

Simone Biles

Simone Biles has been a household name for quite some time for all of the little gymnasts out there. Her medical history was leaked, including the medications she took. She responded honestly and with no shame that her medications were there to treat her for ADHD.

The American gymnastic champion has won nearly 20 gold medals. This is someone that your child can look up to, not only for strength but as a great example of when it's time to pull back. Biles received mixed reactions about withdrawing from part of the Olympics in 2021, but she has stood by her decision as it was, in fact, for her health.

Justin Timberlake

Justin Timberlake has done a lot in the music world. Of course, some hits that come to mind are "Sexyback" and "Can't stop the feeling" from Trolls. Given his wide range, he is a great role model to kids of all ages with ADHD, which he mentioned having in one of his interviews.

Adam Levine

Adam Levine has been vocal about his struggles with ADHD for a long time. He has made it a point, to be honest when talking about ADHD in many interviews and sharing his story, including the highs and lows of having it.

Today, Levine works as one of the coaches on The Voice and is the lead singer of Maroon 5.

Channing Tatum

Here is another individual who hasn't let anything stop him. Channing Tatum's acting credit list is probably as long as a CVS receipt, something he accomplished with ADHD. He has talked about what it's like to have ADHD as a child, and it is something your child might find very relatable!

Emma Watson

What hasn't Emma Watson done with her life? Many young girls idolize young Hermione and her love of books and learning (Seriously, why wasn't she in Ravenclaw again?). The real-life Emma Watson has added a lot more acting credits to her name, including a very notable role as Belle in Beauty and the Beast. And to top it off, she's gotten a degree at Brown University (one of the hardest schools to get into in America) and serves as a United Nations ambassador. Watson still has a lot of life ahead of her, so for those who see her as a role model, it will be interesting to see what she does next!

Micheal Phelps

Micheal Phelps and Biles have a very similar story. Like Biles, Phelps has dedicated his career to being an American olympian athlete. In total, he has won about 23 gold medals, all thanks to his swimming skills. Both he and his mother have talked about his ADHD, saying that swimming has been something in his life that brought him to focus and control. If you have a kiddo struggling right now who is into sports, you never know. At the very least, this could be a model of inspiration for them.

Lisa Ling

There are many reasons that both you and your child could relate to Lisa Ling. Ling is a journalist and often tackles big projects. Her latest was "Our America with Lisa Ling." In it, Ling covered some ADHD topics. Now, if you have ever had a "wait a minute" moment in your life, you might relate to Ling. In doing this project, she noticed several parallels. She got her ADHD diagnosis shortly afterward. Ling is a fantastic example to your kiddo as someone who goes for what she wants and doesn't let the world stop her. Her recent discovery of ADHD and having to deal with this new information suddenly might seem like a familiar story to you.

Will.i.am

Music is a popular path for many with ADHD, and Will.i.am has taken the time to highlight that. He has stated in several interviews that music has helped him cope with ADHD symptoms, among other things, and that when he's in the zone, it clicks. Does your kiddo relate?

Scott Kelly

Many of our examples cover people you might see on a TV screen. Scott Kelly might have been on TV at multiple points in his life, but not the same way the others have.

Growing up, Scott Kelly mentions that his school experience was a mirror image of what someone with ADHD would go through, but they didn't have the diagnosis, so he went undiagnosed. What made him finally get on track was his love for all things space-based. Kelly was able to motivate himself to hyperfocus on school enough to go on and become an astronaut. Today, he is working on getting humans to Mars.

Science is a beautiful yet complicated field. If your little one seems to have a pension for it, this is a great person to point to. Everyone is capable of great things, after all.

Ty Pennington

Some kids rearrange their room 17 times in one year to find the best functionality. If this is your kiddo, they might relate to Ty Pennington.

Pennington is an interior decorator on the show Extreme Makeover: Home Edition. His ADHD is expressed a lot in his job, and he, his mother, his coworkers, and his customers all attest that it is making him very successful.

Karina Smirnoff

Dancing is a popular sport with people everywhere, and many young children enjoy themselves in their dance classes.

If your little one is a dancer, and they get the opportunity to watch Dancing With the Stars, point out Karina Smirnoff. Like many girls with ADHD, this star was diagnosed as an adult. In an interview, she said that her ADHD gives her a lot of energy, and it all goes to her amazing dancing.

Johnny Depp

Depp is an actor who has worn many hats. Literally. Nearly every eccentric children's movie features Johnny Depp, and Depp is Willy Wonka, the Mad Hatter, Captain Jack Sparrow, and more. Not only is it amazing that he has done so much with his life, but he is always on a child's screen.

Richard Branson

Moving away from the stage, it's important to talk about how well people with ADHD can do in the business world. Our first shining example is Sir Richard Branson. His business, Virgin Brand, is everywhere, and it is involved in the health sector, travel sector, banking, space, cell phones, music, etc. Branson has been very public about ADHD, yet he is worth billions today.

Jamie Oliver

Does the name Jamie Oliver sound familiar? If you are anywhere near the UK food scene, it probably will. Oliver is one of the most decorated chefs in the UK, winning awards for his accomplishments. He has been honest about having ADHD, and it doesn't seem to slow him down!

Bill Gates

I absolutely had to throw this name in here. Bill Gates invented Microsoft. That sentence alone speaks for itself. However, his journey wasn't an easy one and included dropping out of Harvard. Sometimes unique ideas can be constrained in school, making it hard to know what you might be capable of. If your kiddo is struggling, as many do, let them know that they don't have to be exceptional in a classroom to succeed in life. Many people don't do it that way.

Role models are always crucial to younger kids. They can give them a chance to have something to look up to, an example to follow, or even just a way to know that it's going to be okay on bad days.

ADHD isn't a negative thing. There are negative symptoms, but the rewired brain is full of potential. These are some people who were able to lock on it, and your kiddo might be able to do this as well!

Chapter 8

Teaching Your Child Life Skills

At the end of the day, the goal of raising children is to turn them into happy and successful adults. That sounds great. Right?

ADHD can feel like it puts a bit of a dampener on that, understandably. Hopefully, the last chapter illustrates that might not be the case. Still, there is likely a way to go, and having superpowers with their ADHD doesn't mean they can skip out on basic life skills. So, what does that look like when your kiddo has ADHD?

Activities and Strategies That Can Help

A list for you!

Lists don't just help those who suffer from ADHD! Trying to organize all of the skills someone needs to learn throughout their childhood can feel like a monumental task. If you feel overwhelmed about it, that's understandable. Creating lists can help you get this in front of you in order to develop a plan of what you want to work on.

If you're struggling to find some examples of practical tasks for your kiddo, many online resources outline the age-appropriateness of specific duties.

Once you have a list, give your kiddo an opportunity to choose ones they want to work on first, as it might help with motivation!

Create Activities Out of It

There are many adulting skills that can be fun to learn. One example is cooking, and another is gardening, painting, and decorating are even better examples. All of these can be made into a game or at least made fun.

Let your child cook a dish as long as they are old enough. But, do not stop there. Let them choose the ingredients and pick out the groceries. By following the process, they have more control, and they learn a couple of skills along the way.

Let your child attend to a small garden. Box gardens are a great start. Finally, when it is needed, let them help redecorate their room.

Pay More Attention To What's Working

This one is hard. We want children to know how to do something perfectly. However, if we are too critical from the get-go, they may stop trying altogether. As they start the new task, focus on the things they are doing correctly. Complement those things and leave the issues at the moment. If, after a few months, there isn't much improvement, try moving to a certain phrasing in constructive criticism. As silly as it might sound, avoid using "but." For example, try not to say, "you did really well at this, but…". Instead, try "wow, we're doing really well with this. Parts' A,' and 'B' looks amazing, and we're just missing a tiny part on task 'C.'". This phrasing uses 'and' instead of 'but,' and it points out the issue without being too critical. For children who are struggling with a task, this can help them know what to improve on without being a hit to their motivation.

Achievement Chart

Are you working on a new task right now? Another way to help your child grow in skills without criticism is to have a chart where they move up as their performance improves. This also can help them understand what they still need to work on. Perhaps there is a small prize or the opportunity to do something fun at the end of the day. Charts are also visual, meaning that kiddos with ADHD will have a better time remembering each time they do the task rather than trying to remember your feedback from last time.

Start With Organization Skills ASAP

Generally, the ADHD brain is not the most organized. Now, that's fine, but what sits in our brain may spill into our physical world. Luckily, organization skills can be taught very early and are likely to stick if you do so. When you teach your kiddo about organization skills, let them know that it doesn't have to be perfect, and it just has to make sense to them.

If you are trying to implement this now, start by getting them excited. You can find some great organization pieces at local craft stores, Walmart, Target, a dollar store, and more! Let them pick some items out that they can make use of! Once that's done, help them create a system. Using labels can help it be more visually apparent as well! As they adjust to having an organizational system, try to check in with them about it. See how it's working, how well they are sticking to it, and if there is anything that can be done to improve the system.

Timers

Distractions tend to be around every corner when you have ADHD. You might have given your child the task of sweeping the kitchen and what you've found is that your kiddo made one or two strokes with the broom and is now watching a hummingbird outside (hey, hummingbirds are cool, but we need to stay on task). One thing that can help is a visual timer. Knowing that chores have to be done at a specific time can help prevent distractions, and on really good days, it can potentially engage hyperfocus.

Be Hands-On

The final thing for this section is to be as hands-on as possible. Children with ADHD generally don't do well when they are just told something, and they need further instruction in the form of visual cues and potentially even the chance to do it with you if that is possible.

Our next set of strategies is for those with older kids!

Teenage Based Strategies

The teenage years can be a scary time, especially if your teen has ADHD. Along with going through this development time, you have to think about another frightening thing. Becoming an adult is right around the corner, and as you look at your 13-year-old or even your 16-year-old, it can be hard to imagine. If that thought makes you panic, do not fret. A lot will happen in these next couple of years, and we are going to be here with some tips to help you get through it!

Organization

With teens, organization isn't just about space anymore. Not only do they need to know about organizing their rooms and personal belongings, but knowing how to organize a schedule is going to become a big deal as well! A lot of the same steps will translate. Make it fun. Get a physical planner, or download an online app that can help them! To make it something they can follow visually, use color filters online, or get some colorful pens and highlighters!

Independence

There is going to be a love-hate relationship on all sides when it comes to independence. Some simple forms of cutting off dependence will be things like not being the one to wake them up for school or remind them to do their homework or tell them to do their chores. You might move them over to preparing their own lunch and possibly another meal during the week, and it may be doing their own laundry. Little things like this, where you typically handle the work, will now be up to them. It's a good idea to get the skill in while you are still close by to answer questions.

I know that it is going to be hard to let them do these things, especially when they forget, but these are the things that will help them in life. And when they forget or fail to do something, right now, they are under your roof so that you can help them, and the consequences are minimal.

The Financial Deal

One trait of ADHD is impulsivity, and let's be honest, that can be really bad for a person's budget. Financial intelligence is something they are better to learn under your roof rather than in the world. First of all, if your teen is able to secure a part-time job, particularly one that is active, it can give them a chance to experience structure. If your teen gets to this point, get a hold of some things that will require them to keep a monthly budget. Some basics are car insurance, gas, and a phone bill. Now, you might want to add on a fun thing or two; it could be a streaming service, for example. One great idea that might cater to your child's interests is subscription boxes. These can be whatever you want (books, art supplies, tea, or even things like snacks from across the world). These things give your kiddo something to look forward to while, at the same time, helping them balance a budget. In order to keep the fun stuff, they will need to be financially responsible.

Encourage Various Relationships

Your child should know what a healthy dating relationship is like, and if they naturally start dating someone while still living with you, here is an excellent opportunity to teach them. This also holds true for friendships, family relationships, if there are any diverse examples, and working relationships if they happen to hold a part-time job.

Getting an idea of what relationships should look like now is going to be an excellent idea for any teen, but especially one with any kind of disability. Unfortunately, people with disabilities are more likely to be taken advantage of by other people, so it's great for them to know what a healthy relationship and health boundaries look like.

A Natural Course Of Action

I remember when I woke up late for school, I rushed around to get everything ready and begged my mom to drive me. She did while letting me know that she was disappointed in me and that I was in trouble for sleeping in.

First of all, we all make human mistakes. My mom didn't have to tell me she was disappointed in me. I was already disappointed in myself, and I had let the mistake happen. Thanks to her, I was on time at least.

For a child with ADHD (or any child), this doesn't help much. When things like this happen, there isn't a need to get mad. They likely already know that something is wrong, and in cases like sleeping in, many people silently go through it in their head about what they should do next time to avoid this.

Now, without saying anything, what is going to help the lesson sink in? Letting the natural course of events take place will. If your child is late walking out the door, they are late to school. As harsh as it sounds, wish them luck and send them on their way. Knowing the direct result of the actions will help them avoid the mistake next time. You don't have to be into math to see it.

The Skills

All of the little tips and tricks we have discussed above (for children young and old) will become very important right here!

Increasing Independence

In teens, we mentioned that there are certain things that they might want to take charge of, but what does this look like for young children? There is a certain level of recommended independence and autonomy at each age that a little one has. Following guidance on this can help ensure that your child is ready to enter the real world.

Time

Again, we talked about this with teens, but it applies to kiddos as well, and I want to address that here. Young children will not always understand what time is and how long certain things might take. For example, if they have a homework assignment that they need to do before an extracurricular activity, they might put it off until the last second. Things like this are when tools like timers and natural consequences come into play so that it helps your child understand what time looks like and how much of it they have.

Saving

Financial building blocks are also best taught in stages. Your teen may be paying for a subscription, but your child may know of a toy they want. Children can learn the power of saving starting at a very young age. If there is something that they want, saving up their allowance is a great way to get it and learn while they are at it!

Taking Charge of Their Meds

We haven't talked much about medication purely because that's a conversation that doctors like to have. If your child does take medication, one day, they are going to have to take it on their own. As they get older, try to slowly guide them to where they are in charge of making sure that they take their medications.

Decision-Making Power

Being impulsive is great for a sudden road trip, trying a new restaurant, or a crazy activity like skydiving. It's not okay for ditching class, speeding, or getting in trouble for drinking at a young age.

This area needs additional focus for the lives of those with ADHD. Making decisions is something they are going to do all of their lives, and having a process together to make good ones is going to help!

There are so many skills out there for adulthood, and it's our job to prepare our kids, no matter what. ADHD might mean that you require some new approaches, but you still got this!

Conclusion

I want to reiterate that I understand how this all feels, and I've been in many of the same positions that you are in right now. Thankfully, I found that a lot of these tips were able to work for my daughter and me.

To date, we are not sure what exactly causes ADHD, but we have a few ideas. It's believed to be located in the prefrontal cortex, where the function of many issues inhibited by ADHD tends to occur. Serotonin production seems to have a role in it as well. Serotonin acts as our motivation chemical, and having it not be adequately produced can create a lot of issues with getting tasks done in a timely manner, something that a lot of people with ADHD struggle with.

There are three identified types of ADHD. Inattentive ADHD has more to do with paying attention to the world around them and is more common in girls. Hyperactive-impulsive ADHD involves impulse control, trouble sitting, hyperactivity, and more. This one is more common in boys. Meanwhile, combined-type ADHD sort of meshes the two together, and it's slightly more common in boys than in girls.

There are some different conditions that relate to ADHD. These range from learning disabilities to emotional disorders. Chapter 2 goes into a lot of details about these. Knowing what signs to look for can help you and your kiddo catch and diagnose these early, which will help you to adjust to this new diagnosis and plan some strategies.

A common thing that many parents run into regarding the child and ADHD is severe emotional outbursts. When someone with a typical brain gets angry, their anger flares up, and they might have a tiny moment where they yell at someone, but then the anger signal will fade away. This isn't true for someone with ADHD. Chemicals create emotions in the brain, and sometimes, that anger signal doesn't fade. It just keeps going, flooding your child with too much n emotion that they don't quite know how to control. It is essential to recognize that this isn't your kiddo's fault when this happens. They really can't control these mechanisms in their brain. During the meltdown, it's often best to let them have their moment. Anything said during that point might not be remembered, or it might enrage them further. Trying to punish this behavior will not affect a child with ADHD. There are some other, different strategies that might make a difference, though.

Speaking of punishment and discipline, there are methods that are ideally suited for those who have ADHD, but there are many that are not. Punishment methods may make the problem worse in the long run, and discipline strategies will only work when the behavior is intentional, which a lot of the behaviors displayed in someone with ADHD aren't. There are ways to make sure they understand the message and help them move past incidents and outbursts in a positive and productive manner.

Diet and exercise are important to everyone, but they can have a unique effect on people with ADHD. Exercise can be especially helpful to someone who is hyperactive. Diet plays a significant role in their health, and having a good diet can manage some ADHD symptoms.

The final thing I want to stress in this book is that ADHD is not all bad. People with ADHD have a specific skill set that allows them to be very productive in this world. Not only that, but they seem to be fantastic at coming up with new things and ideas that bring them success. As they grow and develop, allowing them to take full advantage of the things that their ADHD can do for them can help them grow up to be unique and successful human beings.

References

8 Successful people with ADHD you should know about. (2020, January 22). University of the People. https://www.uopeople.edu/blog/8-of-the-worlds-most-successful-people-with-adhd/

19 Activities for kids with ADHD that burn energy and improve focus. (2018, November 26). Meraki Lane. https://www.merakilane.com/19-activities-for-kids-with-adhd-that-burn-energy-and-improve-focus/

ADDitude Editors. (2016, November 28). *Famous people with ADHD.* ADDitude. https://www.additudemag.com/slideshows/famous-people-with-adhd/

ADDitude Editors. (2020, March 25). *Kids bouncing off the walls? These boredom busters fill time gaps with activity.* ADDitude. https://www.additudemag.com/bouncing-off-the-walls-activities-adhd-kids/

ADHD and behavior - tips on how to discipline your child. (n.d.). Supernanny Parenting. Retrieved May 19, 2022, from https://www.supernanny.co.uk/Advice/-/Parenting-Skills/-/Discipline-and-Reward/ADHD-and-behaviour-~-tips-on-how-to-discipline-your-child.aspx

Allen, S., & Psy.D. (2020, March 31). *"Our home can't withstand all of these emotional ADHD explosions!"* ADDitude. https://www.additudemag.com/adhd-control-emotions-parent/

American Academy of Child and Adolescent Psychiatry. (2019). *ADHD & the brain.* Aacap.org. https://www.aacap.org/AACAP/Families_and_Youth/Facts_for_Families/FFF-Guide/ADHD_and_the_Brain-121.aspx

Anderson, J. (2021, April 13). *The effect of spanking on the brain.* Harvard Graduate School of Education.

References

https://www.gse.harvard.edu/news/uk/21/04/effect-spanking-brain

August 11, G. M., & 2020. (2020). *How to help kids with attention and learning issues with remote, hybrid, or in-Person learning.* Parents. https://www.parents.com/health/add-adhd/how-parents-can-help-children-with-attention-and-learning-issues-with-remote-hybrid-or-in-person-learning/

Brown, T. (n.d.). *ADHD and emotions.* Www.understood.org. https://www.understood.org/en/articles/adhd-and-emotions-what-you-need-to-know

Brown, T. (2016, November 29). *Exaggerated emotions: how and why ADHD triggers intense feelings.* ADDitude. https://www.additudemag.com/slideshows/adhd-emotions-understanding-intense-feelings/

Carpenter, D. (2006, October 6). *Never punish a child for behavior outside his control.* ADDitude. https://www.additudemag.com/behavior-punishment-parenting-child-with-adhd/

CDC. (2019, August 27). *Other Concerns and Conditions with concerns and conditions associated with ADHD.* Centers for Disease Control and Prevention. https://www.cdc.gov/ncbddd/adhd/conditions.html

Chronister, D. K., & Program, K. T. T. T. (2021, June 19). *Best activities for teens with ADHD* Key Transitions. https://keytransitions.com/activities-for-teens-with-adhd/

Cohen, M. (2018). *Can you treat ADHD without drugs?* WebMD. https://www.webmd.com/add-adhd/childhood-adhd/can-you-treat-adhd-without-drugs#:~:text=Exercise

Crawford, J. (2018, April 25). *Parenting tips for ADHD: 21 ways to help.* Www.medicalnewstoday.com. https://www.medicalnewstoday.com/articles/321621#twenty-one-parenting-tips

Facts about saturated fats: MedlinePlus Medical Encyclopedia. (2020). Medlineplus.gov. https://medlineplus.gov/ency/patientinstructions/000838.htm#:~:text=Saturated%20fat%20is%20a%20type

Healthline. (2013). *What are the three types of ADHD?* Healthline. https://www.healthline.com/health/adhd/three-types-adhd

Kessler, Z. (2013, October 26). *The secret to no-shout, no-tears discipline.* ADDitude. https://www.additudemag.com/discipline-without-yelling-calm-parenting-for-kids-with-adhd/

Kris. (2019). *25+ strategies for kids with ADHD.* Pathways 2 Success. https://www.thepathway2success.com/25-strategies-for-kids-with-adhd/

Legume basics. (n.d.). Www.dvo.com. http://www.dvo.com/recipe_pages/betty/LEGUME_BASICS.php

Leonard, J. (2019, May 31). *ADHD diet: Best foods, foods to avoid, and meal plans.* Www.medicalnewstoday.com. https://www.medicalnewstoday.com/articles/325352#foods-to-limit-or-avoid

Marcy. (2016, November 1). *How to teach life skills to your teen with ADHD.* Ben and Me. https://www.benandme.com/teaching-life-skills-teen-with-adhd/

Myers, R. (n.d.-a). *10 concentration and focus building techniques for children with ADHD.* Empowering Parents. https://www.empoweringparents.com/article/5-simple-concentration-building-techniques-for-kids-with-adhd/

Myers, R. (n.d.-b). *Effective consequences for ADHD kids.* Empowering Parents. Retrieved May 19, 2022, from https://www.empoweringparents.com/article/effective-consequences-for-adhd-kids/

Norton, A. (2021). *Science reveals how red meat harms the heart.* WebMD. https://www.webmd.com/heart-disease/news/20211229/science-reveals-how-red-meat-harms-the-heart

Parekh, R. (2017, July). *What is ADHD?* American Psychiatric Association; American Psychiatric Association. https://www.psychiatry.org/patients-families/adhd/what-is-adhd

Sherrell, Z. (2021, July 21). *What are the benefits of ADHD?* Www.medicalnewstoday.com.

https://www.medicalnewstoday.com/articles/adhd-benefits#adhd-superpowers

Tacoma, N. (2019, March 11). *Mindfulness and ADHD: 4 relaxation games for children.* ImpactParents. https://impactparents.com/blog/adhd/mindfulness-and-adhd-4-relaxation-games-for-children/

Watson, S. (2016). ADHD: *7 life skills your teen should master.* WebMD. https://www.webmd.com/add-adhd/childhood-adhd/features/adhd-life-skills

Watson, S. (2021, February 8). *21 ways to make lemonade during the sourest times.* ADDitude. https://www.additudemag.com/activities-for-kids-with-adhd-skills-pandemic/

Whelan, C. (2021, April 12). *8 ADHD meditation & mindfulness tips.* Healthline. https://www.healthline.com/health/adhd/adhd-meditation#tune-out-noises